TWAYNE'S WORLD AUTHORS SERIES

A Survey of the World's Literature

Sylvia E. Bowman, Indiana University

GENERAL EDITOR

FRANCE

Maxwell A. Smith, Guerry Professor of French, Emeritus
The University of Chattanooga
Former Visiting Professor in Modern Languages
The Florida State University

EDITOR

Saint-John Perse

(TWAS 244)

TWAYNE'S WORLD AUTHORS SERIES (TWAS)

The purpose of TWAS is to survey the major writers —novelists, dramatists, historians, poets, philosophers, and critics—of the nations of the world. Among the national literatures covered are those of Australia, Canada, China, Eastern Europe, France, Germany, Greece, India, Italy, Japan, Latin America, the Netherlands, New Zealand, Poland, Russia, Scandinavia, Spain, and the African nations, as well as Hebrew, Yiddish, and Latin Classical literatures. This survey is complemented by Twayne's United States Authors Series and English Authors Series.

The intent of each volume in these series is to present a critical-analytical study of the works of the writer; to include biographical and historical material that may be necessary for understanding, appreciation, and critical appraisal of the writer and to present all material in clear, concise English—but not to vitiate the scholarly content of the work by doing so.

Saint-John Perse

By RENÉ GALAND

Wellesley College

Twayne Publishers, Inc.   ::   New York

Preface

For nearly half a century, Saint-John Perse's literary fame hardly extended beyond a relatively small circle of readers. And yet, he must have found in their admiration the highest reward which a poet could desire, since this elite included Claudel, Valéry, Gide, Proust, Rilke, Ungaretti, T. S. Eliot, James Joyce, Hugo von Hofmannsthal, Jorge Guillén, Valery Larbaud, Léon-Paul Fargue, André Breton, René Char, Stephen Spender, W. H. Auden, Archibald MacLeish, Allen Tate—and the list is far from complete. The American Academy and the National Institute of Arts and Letters were the first official bodies to give public recognition to his work: in 1950, Saint-John Perse received the quinquennial Award of Merit Medal for Poetry. With the award, in 1959, of the *Grand prix national des Lettres* and the *Grand prix international de Poésie,* and of the Nobel Prize for Literature in 1960, his fame in the world of letters received the ultimate consecration.

The poetry of Saint-John Perse holds a special appeal for American readers. He is, to be sure, a native of the New World, and it was in America that he sought refuge during the dark days of World War II. From 1940 to 1957, he made his home in the United States. It was only in 1957 that he returned to France to take possession of his new residence on the Mediterranean coast. His choice of an Anglo-Saxon pseudonym may be indicative of an early interest in America. His friend Valery Larbaud, in his early works, had assumed the poetic identity of A. O. Barnabooth, the son of an American multimillionaire. Saint-John Perse may well have been influenced by this example.[1] His first discovery of the United States took place in 1921, when he returned from his post at the French Legation in Peking by way of Japan and America. An important part of his leave was devoted to a visit of the West Coast from Mexico to Canada. It was in America, during his years of exile, that he wrote most of his major poems, and the American scene plays an essential role in these works. There is, in the *Poem to a Foreign Lady,* a vivid evocation of a Washington summer, with its locusts, its fireflies, its mocking birds, and its cardinals. *Snows* brings to the reader the vision of New York City with its snow-covered skyscrapers. *Winds* ranges over the American continent from the Gulf of Mexico to the Pacific. Deserted plantations with their tall columns, Spanish moss hanging from ancient trees, wide rivers slowly making their way to the sea through silted estuaries, marshlands where alligators dig their underwater burrows, and alluvial islands peopled with snakes compose a striking vision of the Deep South. The Far West is represented by deep canyons and arid mesas where horsemen ride over the dead debris of the past, potsherds and animal bones, or where uranium prospectors listen to their Geiger counters. *Winds* also spans the history of America, from the Spanish conquistadores to the nuclear scientists of Los Alamos.

American readers of Saint-John Perse enjoy the distinct advantage of having at their disposal the magnificent bilingual editions sponsored by the Bollingen Foundation.[2] It must be recognized, however, that no translation, whatever its excellence, can convey the range of meaning suggested by the original poem. My main purpose, in this book, has been to provide the interpretation required to recognize and appreciate the full evocative power of Saint-John Perse's poetry. I believe that this goal can best be achieved through a study of his poems as discrete symbolic structures. From *Pictures for Crusoe* to *Chronicle,* each poem published by Saint-John Perse is characterized by its own theme, its distinctive setting, and its singular imagery. These interpretations stress the elements from which the poetry of Saint-John Perse derives its essential power: his vision of human destiny and the symbolic patterns which embody this vision. The concluding chapter is a general presentation of his theory of poetry. I have attempted to define the deep relationship which links together the poet's metaphysical concept of Being, his psychological understanding of artistic creation, his dominant themes and motifs, his selection of images and symbols, and the formal structures of his poetic language.

All the quotations are given in English as they appear in the Bollingen editions. The only exceptions are those required to

Preface

illustrate significant differences between the translation and the original or the poet's use of rhythm and sound. In the case of texts which have not been translated into English, the version given is my own. The chronology which follows is based on the authorized biography given in Jacques Charpier's *Saint-John Perse*, which covers the years 1887–1961. Documentation concerning the years 1961–72 has been generously communicated by Madame Claudine Chonez, Professor Arthur Knodel, of the University of Southern California, and Professor Daniel Racine, of Howard University, whose assistance is gratefully acknowledged here. I also wish to thank Wellesley College for its generous award of a research grant for the preparation of this publication.

Acknowledgments

Excerpts from *Anabasis* by St.-John Perse translated by T. S. Eliot are reprinted by permission of Harcourt Brace Jovanovich, Inc.; copyright 1938, 1949, by Harcourt Brace Jovanovich, Inc.; copyright, 1966, by Esme Valerie Eliot.

Excerpts from the following works are reprinted by permission of Princeton University Press: *Eloges and other Poems*, by St.-John Perse, translated by Louise Varèse, Bollingen Series LV (copyright © 1956 by Bollingen Foundation); *Exile*, by St.-John Perse, translated by Denis Devlin, Bollingen Series XV (copyright © 1949 by Bollingen Foundation); *Winds*, by St.-John Perse, translated by Hugh Chisholm, Bollingen Series XXXIV (copyright © 1953 by Bollingen Foundation); *Seamarks*, by St.-John Perse, translated by Wallace Fowlie, Bollingen Series LXVIII (copyright © 1958 by Bollingen Foundation); *Chronique*, by St.-John Perse, translated by Robert Fitzgerald, Bollingen Series LXIX (copyright © 1961 by Bollingen Foundation); *Two Addresses*, by St.-John Perse, *On Poetry*, translated by W. H. Auden, and *Dante*, translated by Robert Fitzgerald, Bollingen Series LXXXVI (copyright © 1966 by Bollingen Foundation); St.-John Perse, *Collected Poems*, also copyright © 1971 by Princeton University Press.

The photograph of St.-John Perse is reproduced by permission of Dorothy Norman and the Philadelphia Museum of Art.

Contents

Contents

Chronology

1887– Birth of Marie-René-Alexis Saint-Leger Leger on the islet
1899 of Saint-Léger-les-Feuilles (Guadeloupe). Both parents
were descended from families established on the island
since the eighteenth century. Childhood spent in Pointe-à-
Pitre, on the islet of Saint-Léger-les-Feuilles, and on the
two family plantations. Studies at the *Lycée* of Pointe-à-
Pitre (1896–99).

1899– The entire family moves to Pau (France) where Alexis
1904 Leger completes his *baccalauréat*. Friendship with the
French poet Francis Jammes.

1904 Enters the Law School of the University of Bordeaux. Also
interested in Greek, philosophy, science, and medicine.
Writes *Pictures for Crusoe*.

1905– Friendship with Paul Claudel. After one year of military
1907 service, resumes his law studies. Writes the poem "*Des
Villes sur trois modes*" (1906) and the first poems of
Praises (1907).

1908– Completes his law studies while pursuing his interest in
1910 philosophy, anthropology, and music. Publication of "*Des
Villes sur trois modes*" in the review *Pan* (1908) and of
Praises in *La Nouvelle Revue Française* (1909–10). Friendship with the poet and critic Valery Larbaud.

1911 Publication of *Praises* in book form. Meeting with André
Gide. Decides to prepare for the foreign service examination.

1912 Study trip in England. Meeting with Joseph Conrad, G. K.
Chesterton, Hilaire Belloc, Arnold Bennett, Rabindranath
Tagore. In Paris, where he continues his studies, friend-
ship with Paul Valéry.

1913 Study trip to England and Germany, where he meets with
the German poet Richard Dehmel.

1914– Friendship with Satie and Stravinsky. After passing the

1916 foreign service examination, serves first as attaché to the Cabinet of the minister of foreign affairs, then as attaché to the Foreign Press Service.

1916– Sent to the French legation in Peking. Travels in Man-
1921 churia, Korea, Mongolia, and the Gobi Desert. *Anabasis* dates from this period.

1921– Returns to France by way of Japan, Hawaii, the South
1922 Pacific, and America. Attends the International Conference on the Limitation of Armaments held in Washington. Meeting with Aristide Briand, who is impressed by his intelligence and his ability.

1922– Serves at the Ministry of Foreign Affairs (Asia-Pacific
1925 Section). Publication of poems in various reviews, some unsigned, others under the signature "St-J. Perse": a *Poem for Valery Larbaud* (1922), extracts from *Anabasis* (1922–24), *Friendship of the Prince, Song of the Heir Presumptive,* and an adaptation of T. S. Eliot's *The Hollow Men* (1924). Only the "Letter to Jacques Rivière," in the memorial issue of *La Nouvelle Revue Française* devoted to this author (1925), is signed "A. Saint-Léger Léger." Revised and expanded edition of *Praises.*

1925– Promoted to the post of cabinet director by Aristide Briand,
1932 then minister of foreign affairs. Voluntary withdrawal from all public forms of literary activity.

1933– Promoted to the rank of ambassador and appointed secre-
1939 tary general for foreign affairs. A confirmed anti-Nazi, Alexis Leger resists the appeasement policy which culminates in the Munich Conference.

1940 On May 19, his political enemies succeed in having him removed from his post of secretary general. In view of the circumstances, Alexis Leger declines the offer of an appointment as ambassador to Washington and requests to be relieved from all duties. On June 16, leaves France aboard a British freighter bound for England. Decides to seek refuge in America, where he settles in New York. The collaborationist Vichy government deprives him of his French nationality, confiscates his property, and expels him from the Order of the Legion of Honor. The Gestapo ransacks his Paris apartment and destroys his unpublished manuscripts.

1941   Accepts an appointment as Fellow of the Library of Congress, with the title of consultant in French literature, after ascertaining that this position involves no direct subsidy from the U.S. government. Writes the poem *Exile* on Long Beach Island (New Jersey), and the "Letter to Archibald MacLeish."

1942   Commemorative speech in honor of Aristide Briand given at New York University. Writes the poem *Rains* near Savannah, Georgia. First publication of *Exile* and of the "Letter to Archibald MacLeish."

1943   Writes the *Poem to a Foreign Lady* in Washington (first publication the same year). First publication of *Rains*.

1944   Writes the poem *Snows* in New York City (first publication the same year). After the liberation of France is fully reinstated in all his rights and privileges as a French citizen and a member of the Foreign Service. First publication of the collected poems *Exile, Poem to a Foreign Lady, Rains,* and *Snows* under the title *Quatre poèmes (1941–1944)*.

1945   Completes the poem *Winds*. First publication of the short poem *Lullaby*. Second edition of the collected poems *Exile, Poem to a Foreign Lady, Rains,* and *Snows* under the title *Exile*.

1946   First publication of the poem *Winds*.

1948   First publication of a fragment of *Seamarks* (Canto VIII of the "Strophe"). Third edition of *Praises* (expanded).

1950   Officially retires from the French Foreign Service with the rank of ambassador. Receives the Award of Merit Medal for Poetry. Publication of the "Invocation" of *Seamarks*.

1951   Contribution to the memorial issue of *La Nouvelle Revue Française* in honor of André Gide.

1952   Tribute to Valery Larbaud. Publication of the "Dedication" of *Seamarks*.

1953   Publication, in Paris, of *oeuvre poétique I*. This first volume of his collected poems includes *Praises, The Glory of Kings, Anabasis, Exile,* and *Winds*. The poems grouped under the collective title *The Glory of Kings* were included in the previous editions of *Praises*.

1954   Tribute to the poet and dramatist Schéhadé.

1955   Contribution to the memorial issue of *La Nouvelle Revue Française* in honor of Paul Claudel.

1956   Tribute to Adrienne Monnier. Publication of the "Strophe" (Canto IX) of *Seamarks*.

1957   Publication of *Seamarks*. Contribution to the memorial issue of *La Nouvelle Revue Française* in honor of Valery Larbaud. First return to France since 1940 to take possession of his new residence on the Mediterranean coast, on the Presqu'île de Giens. From 1957 to 1967, Saint-John Perse spends five months of each year in France (late spring to late fall).

1958   Marriage to Dorothy Russell, *née* Milburn.

1959   Letter to a Swedish writer on the thematic structure of *Seamarks*. First publication of *Chronicle*. Awards: *Grand prix national des Lettres, Grand prix international de Poésie*, honorary membership in the Modern Language Association, honorary doctorate from Yale University.

1960   Nobel Prize for Literature. Tribute to Giuseppe Ungaretti. Publication of the revised edition, in two volumes, of his collected poems.

1961   Publication of the Nobel Prize acceptance speech (*Poésie*). Tribute to Rabindranath Tagore.

1962   Original edition of *L'Ordre des Oiseaux*, with twelve color etchings by Georges Braque. Tribute to J. L. Borges.

1963   Essay on Léon-Paul Fargue. Contribution to the fiftieth-anniversary issue of *Les Cahiers du Sud*. Tribute to the memory of President Kennedy.

1964   Contribution to the memorial issue of *Derrière le Miroir* in honor of Georges Braque. Tribute to Mrs. Jacqueline Kennedy.

1965   Inaugural address at the International Congress in Florence for the seventh centenary of Dante. Publication of *Honneur à Saint-John Perse*.

1967   Permanent residence at the Presqu'île de Giens.

1969   Publication of the poem *Chanté par Celle qui fut là* . . . (fragment of a much longer poem).

1971   Public statement in honor of Igor Stravinsky on the occasion of the composer's death. Contribution to the special issue of *Les Cahiers de L'Herne* in honor of René Char. Publication of the short poem *Chant pour un équinoxe*.

CHAPTER 1

The Lost Eden

IN the collected poems of Saint-John Perse, three early works have been gathered under the single title *Praises: To Celebrate a Childhood,* dated 1907; *Praises,* dated 1908; and *Pictures for Crusoe,* written in 1904, when the author was only seventeen. An introductory poem bears the apposite title *Written on the Door.* All of these poems draw their inspiration from the author's childhood, but it should be noted that *Pictures for Crusoe,* the first written, is the least personal and perhaps the most richly symbolic.

I *Pictures for Crusoe*

Pictures for Crusoe is the earliest work retained in the collected poetry of Saint-John Perse. The achievement is indeed impressive. The composition, the diction, the tone, the imagery, the use of sound and rhythm, all reveal that the author, at the age of seventeen, had already forged his own unmistakable idiom. As the title indicates, the poem consists of a series of pictures representing nine scenes from the life of Robinson Crusoe in his old age. Robinson, as the adolescent poet imagines him, is back in England, presumably in London since there are possible references to the towers of Westminster and to the Thames. The nine *Pictures for Crusoe* are built along the same structure: the contrast, expressed or implied, between the lost Island and the City which is Robinson's present abode.

The opening lines of the first section, "The Bells," convey Robinson's mood with a sure sense of feeling: "Old man with naked hands,/cast up among men again, Crusoe!/you wept, I imagine, when from the Abbey towers, like a tide, the sob of the bells poured over the City . . . /O Despoiled!" The selection of details and the use of imagery give admirable proof of the poet's craftsmanship. Robinson, who once was young and single master of his

17

kingdom, now is only a man among other men, aging and weeping over his loss. An analogy is suggested between the flow of his tears and the flow of sound issuing from the Abbey towers, between the sadness of the man and the melancholy tolling of the bells. The French word *flux* has the double meaning of "flood tide" and "discharge from an infected wound." The sobbing of the bells and the old man's tears thus appear as a sign of disease. Another comparison is later suggested between the sound flowing from the bells and the music of the tide on the island shore. The analogy actually reinforces the contrast between the tainted sounds spreading over the City and the pure music of the tropical sea, "the strange music that is born and is muffled under the folded wing of the night,/like the linked circles that are the waves of a conch. . . ."

This closing image of "The Bells" is modulated into the opening verse of the following section, "The Wall": "The stretch of wall is across the way to break the circle of your dream." The city wall looms as a threatening presence against which the old man's dream cries out in alarm. Can the dreamer escape the corruption which surrounds him? Everything around him is soiled: the grandfather's chair against which he rests his head is greasy with dirt, and his mouth has been defiled by the greasy taste of cooking fat. The memory of the Island rises before him as a pure vision: the green light of dawn emerging from the mysterious waters, the pungent smell of mangroves, the musky honey of ants, the taste of green fruit souring the dawn, the air spiced with the salt of the trade winds. The vision ends on a climax of exultation: "Joy! O joy set free in the heights of the sky! Pure linens are resplendent, invisible parvises are strewn with grasses and leaves, and the green delights of the earth are painted on the century of a long day. . . ." The dreamer has become a seer: he has overcome the wall of reality and reconquered the lost Eden where everything was free from taint or defilement, when the passage of time posed no threat to human joy. The heavenly character of this vision is subtly brought out by the word "parvis," which has the same etymology as "paradise."

The third section, "The City," develops the theme of corruption stated in "The Wall." The air that men must breathe over and over again is foul with greasy smoke. It has the smell of uncleanness and death. The description of the City, as evening falls, creates a bleak atmosphere of poverty, filth, sadness, repression, and decay. A climax is reached in a powerful image which likens the City to a huge abscess suppurating into the sea through the river. The City is diseased and polluted. The Island, on the other hand, is untainted and life-giving. It appears as a feminine figure fecundated by the oceans. On the Island, everything is teeming with life, and the urge of life to reproduce itself can be perceived everywhere: in the tangled flight of mosquitoes, in the gentle calls of crickets, in the pure song of lizards, in the swirling waters where death is challenged and abiding faith in life is proclaimed: "Corollas, mouths of watered silks: mourning that breaks and blossoms! Big moving flowers on a journey, flowers alive forever, and that will not cease to grow throughout the world. . . ." In the silent tropical night, all is unity and harmony. A sleeping bird, calm waters, swaying palms: all is peace and ecstatic repose. No sign of a human presence mars the perfection of this lost Eden. The triumphant cry which concludes "The Wall" is repeated here, but this section of the poem ends on a different note. With his face "proffered to the signs of the night like an upturned palm," Robinson appears as a supplicant rather than a victor.

The five sections which follow have a single theme: whatever comes from the Island is corrupted or destroyed by the City. On the Island, Friday knelt timidly. Out of gratitude for the man who saved his life, he pledged his allegiance, he acknowledged Robinson's suzerainty. In the City, he is a servant. He wears a cast-off livery and his eyes are full of deceit. Once he was close to the things of the earth. He laughed in the sun and moved in the light the blue streaming of his limbs. Now his laughter is depraved, he drinks the oil of lamps, steals from the larder, and lusts for the skirts of the cook who is fat and smells of fish. The parrot is a pitiful substitute for Robinson's pet on the Island. The City has made him diseased and unclean. The goatskin parasol lies in the attic dust, next to the cat litter. The bow has burst open along the whole length of its secret fiber, like a dead pod. The seed brought from the Island has not sprouted. Everything suggests neglect, corruption, defilement, disintegration, sterility, and death.

In *Pictures for Crusoe*, the youthful author is undoubtedly expressing his nostalgia for the happy years of his childhood. The aging Crusoe is the alter ego of the young law student at the University of Bordeaux, but the individual experience of loss and exile is lifted to the level of the universal through the use of this poetic persona. The *tu* form with which the speaker of the poem addresses Robinson implies both familiarity and detachment. It must be noted, however, that in *Pictures for Crusoe,* Saint-John Perse gives its first poetic expression to a fundamental theme in his works: the sense of historical becoming, the feeling that youth has to give way to old age, that the City must win over the Island. When he contrasts the City and the Island, he is also contrasting two ways of life, two patterns of culture, two stages in the evolution of mankind. Robinson on his island appears as a symbol of the preindustrial age, of a time when the social structure remains feudal, when the economy is predominantly agricultural, when life still follows the rhythms of nature. *Pictures for Crusoe* is a ringing denunciation of the destruction wrought by the industrial revolution. Men are either masters or servants: innocence is no longer possible. When Friday has to wear the red livery which brands him a servant, his soul becomes that of a servant. The City is the Waste Land where nothing can germinate or bear fruit, a prison which poisons the body and depraves the soul.

Pictures for Crusoe reflects a deeper, although possibly more obvious, meaning. The archetypal structure of the poem may be expressed in two words: paradise lost. The Island recalls such myths as the fabulous Isles of the Hesperides or the Fortunate Islands. It is quite understandable that the lost Eden, for a native of Guadeloupe, should be associated with the engram of the Island. According to some psychoanalysts, the island is Woman, the giver of life. In *Pictures for Crusoe,* the Island does indeed appear as a *locus amoenus,* as the mythical image of Mother Nature, and the poet's nostalgia reflects the yearning of modern man for the *illud tempus,* for the mythical age when man lived free from corruption and death.

The final section of the poem, "The Book," takes on an added meaning in the light of these considerations. The wailing wind in the hearth, one evening, as long rains march toward the City, provokes Robinson's lament. In the awesome spectacle of primeval nature, Robinson once communed with a numinous presence. On the Island, the Lord spoke unto him: has He forsaken His creature? In the darkened City, Robinson no longer feels the nearness of the Sacred. The divine vision which once was granted him

grows fainter and fainter. A sequence is indicated by the development of the poem: in the first three sections, the power of the
dream enables Robinson to resurrect the lost glory, however
briefly. Then come the sections dominated by disease, sterility,
and death. The dream has lost its power. The vision is gone. In
the final section, Robinson turns to the prophecies of the Sacred
Book. The Book does not bring back the vision, but it promises its
return: "sitting by the window opposite the stretch of wall across
the way, having failed to resuscitate the lost splendour,/you
would open the Book,/and letting your worn finger wander
among the prophecies, your gaze far away, you awaited the moment of departure, the rising of the great wind that would suddenly tear you away, like the typhoon, parting the clouds before
your waiting eyes." A number of hackneyed quotations come to
mind: *"Levez-vous vite, orages désirés . . .";* *"Emportez-moi
comme elle, orageux aquilons!";* "Oh! lift me as a wave, a leaf, a
cloud!" [1] There is, however, no triteness in the young poet's
imagery. The French word *desceller* (to tear away) carries a connotation of brute power. It also means "to break the seals" and
suggests the liberating power of the great wind. Besides its common meaning of tropical storm, the word "typhoon" is reminiscent
of the Egyptian god Typhon, who killed his brother Osiris and cut
his body into pieces. The scattered remnants were later reunited
and brought back to life. Destruction was but a prelude to regeneration and rebirth. Similarly, the old man whose worn finger wanders among the prophecies hopes that death will restore him to his
former estate.

Saint-John Perse has recounted how, when he was only thirteen
years old, Claudel attempted to convert him to the Catholic faith.
During Claudel's demonstration, a violent storm broke out and
distracted the youth, who paid more attention to the changing
shapes and colors of the clouds or to the sight of trees buffeted by
the wind than to Claudel's theological reasoning. Thunder and
lightning made a stronger impression than the philosophy of Saint
Thomas or the arguments of Saint Anselm. They were a direct
revelation of the god hidden in the heart of things. As he told of
this childhood episode to the French poet Claude Vigée, Saint-
John Perse concluded: "The divine fire appeared to me in the immediate world. I had no need of any other mediator than the very

elements which make up our universe. This is the reason why I
never could feel quite a Christian: like all true children of the
Islands, *I am saved from birth.*" [2]

The closing section of *Pictures for Crusoe* thus suggests an intriguing connection between religion and literature. The wailing
wind in the hearth has stirred in Robinson's heart "the obscure
birth of speech" (*l'obscure naissance du langage*). Language is
born when the sacred presence is no more and when the dream
has lost its power to bring it back. The Book is that which must
take the place of the absent God. It comes on the scene when the
primeval bond between man and God has been broken and can
no longer be restored, when the dream fails to resurrect the lost
splendor. The Book does not resurrect it either: it only testifies to
its loss. It is the paradox of literature that it must manifest the
presence of Being by denouncing its absence. I find it significant
that the author of *Pictures for Crusoe,* when he experienced this
loss, did not turn to *the* Book, but to *a* book, specifically, *Robinson
Crusoe.* To Robinson, the Bible offers a mythic model which
enables him to transcend his fate and to face deprivation and
death. The book *Robinson Crusoe* may well have fulfilled a similar function for an adolescent poet. In the absence of religious
faith, he may have found in Defoe's novel a disguised mythical
model. Robinson's island is a modern version of the lost Eden. It
does not spark the hope of religious salvation, but it remains as a
nostalgia creative of new values. When religious myths no longer
speak to the heart of man, literary myths must take over some of
their functions.[3]

II *To Celebrate a Childhood*

To Celebrate a Childhood glorifies the wonder of life as it revealed itself to a child on the Antilles. Like *Pictures for Crusoe,*
the six sections of this poem present a series of scenes from the
poet's early years. *Pictures for Crusoe* is a transposition of his experience, *To Celebrate a Childhood* is its direct expression. It has
been noted, with good justification, that "everything described in
the poem is authentic. It is pure autobiography. . . ." I would,
however, qualify the critic's conclusion that "there is no fantasy
and very little 'fabulation' in Perse." [4] The experience related in
To Celebrate a Childhood is undoubtedly authentic, but its truth
is intensely subjective. A child's mental universe retains the basic

structure of archaic thought. Only a poet can recapture the sense of magic which colors the child's vision of his world. What impresses me most, in *To Celebrate a Childhood,* is precisely the poet's power of "fabulation," taking the word in its original meaning of "mythopoeic." I believe this is why he alludes to his "fabulous eyelids" (II): they opened on a world of wonder. In a similar fashion, sunlight is perceived as a mythical hero whose exploits open up for the child the kingdom of poetic vision (I).

The world, as it appears to the child, is experienced as a totality. Its unity and continuity are not intellectual concepts. They are sensuously felt: "In those days they bathed you in water-of-green-leaves; and the water was of green sun too; and your mother's maids, tall glistening girls, moved their warm legs near you who trembled . . ." (I). The water is green from the leaves; it is also warm and bright like the sun which shines upon it. The sun, in its turn, appears to be green like the leaves.[5] The maids, who are glistening and warm, have these attributes in common with the sun and the water. The world is not fragmented or divided into clear-cut categories: human, animal, vegetal, and mineral. The nurse's mouth has the taste of rose apples, flowers end in parrot calls, and beasts which feed on roots, like men, grow to partake of a nobler essence. Sensations merge in the "dark and deep unity" described by Baudelaire in his celebrated sonnet *Correspondances.* The buzzing of flies is "as though the light had sung" and "the hour of noon is more sonorous than a mosquito." Sea, land, and sky exchange places. The sea appears "tiered like a sky above orchards" or as "pale meadows" on which fabulous creatures walk.

It is, of course, the lack of clear-cut divisions which renders possible the child's magic vision of the world. The primitive cosmogony of a black sorcerer finds a ready believer in the child who listens to his solemn pronouncements (II). The tall white forms carried by his father's boat could well be "wind-blown angels" rather than "wholesome men dressed in good linen with pith helmets." Primitive men saw gods in the sky and in the stars, in thunder and lightning, in stormy seas or high mountains. The child retains the visionary powers of archaic men whose imagination created theogonies: "For in the morning, on the pale meadows of the naked Water, all along the West, I saw Princes walking, and their Kinsmen, all well dressed and silent, because the sea before noon is a Sunday where sleep has taken on the body of

a God bending his knees" (VI). Nature reveals her mysteries:
"And torches, at noon, were raised for my flights./And I believe
that Arches, Halls of ebony and tin were lighted every evening at
the dream of the volcanoes,/at the hour when our hands were
joined before the idol in gala robes" (VI). The "idol in gala robes"
may refer to a statue of Jesus and the Virgin Mary, to whom the
child had to address his evening prayers, but the use of the word
"idol" suggests a more primitive cult. As he joined his hands in
prayer, he had perhaps the vision of secret temples and sanctu-
raries lighted up in the "dream of the volcanoes," which could be
interpreted as manifestations of the awesome power of Nature.[6]
But Nature in all her might is not the child's master: she is his
servant (II).

This attitude, at least to some extent, may reflect the child's
social position. As the son of a plantation owner, he probably
established an analogy between the organization of his family
plantations and the order of nature. The entire world was a place
where things were made "for children's dreams" (III). Spontaneously, the child relived the myth of Adam in the garden of Eden
when the first man was given power over all living creatures and
gave them names: "Naming each thing, I proclaimed that it was
great, naming each beast, that it was beautiful and good" (II).
His enthusiastic praise encompasses the entire range of his experience. Adam disobeyed the Lord, but the child does not rebel
against the laws of his world. He recognizes that it is forbidden to
kill the hummingbird with a stone, or that a certain maidservant is
entitled to a chair when indoors. He accepts the loss of a baby-
sister without question, let alone rebellion, as he accepts the death
of his most beautiful insects, eaten by carnivorous flowers. His
acceptance goes so far as to find beauty in suffering and death
(II). He even gives praise to his own tears and fears, to his own
suffering and sorrow, to the "night sweats," to the midnights "un-
real with fever and with a taste of cisterns" (V). In the kingdom
of childhood, joy and sorrow, health and sickness, life and death,
darkness and light are united in the ecstasy of being. In its harmony, the reconciliation of opposites comes nearer to its realization: "everything was glimmering realms and frontiers of light.
And shade and light in those days were more nearly the same
thing" (III).

The child has known suffering, he has seen death. Can he, however, relate the death of his baby-sister to his own? Does he know the terror of time? He has not felt his "limbs grow and wax heavy, nourished with age" (III). He does not fully realize that what has been, shall be no more. A falling fruit does not remind him of his own mortality (III). The "white kingdom" of childhood is an enchanted kingdom, a dreamlike world into which the child led, "perhaps, a body without shadow" (I). Bodies which cast no shadow transcend reality and are not subject to its laws. They know no becoming, only an eternal present. Freedom from time is also suggested by the juxtaposition of opposites. The magic world of childhood is both primeval and fresh. It combines "the sweetness/of an oldness of roots" (I) and the "rawness of an evening with an odour of Deluge" (VI). The motif of the Flood suggests purification and regeneration. The world makes a new beginning. It is intensely alive and strives for the perfection of its own essence. Nature possesses the boundless fecundity and the creative energy of mythical origins (I).

The entire poem thus appears as an attempt to recapture the lost dream in all its richness and its singularity. As he lists the persons, the creatures, the objects or the scenes of his childhood, the poet seems to be torn between the wish not to overlook any single element and the desire to dwell lovingly upon each marvel preserved in the treasure house of his memory. Two stylistic techniques are extensively used to satisfy these contradictory impulses: enumeration and repetition. The poem reads at times like an inventory, and the reader is left with the impression of a world so full of wonders that it would be impossible to list them all (III). Repetition, on the other hand, is used to emphasize those moments which left a deeper impression on the child. The echoes which reverberate throughout the poem also emphasize the feeling of continuity, of duration, of permanence. In a sense, the entire poem is a "repetition" of the lost past. In religion as well as in magic, repetition forms the basis of ritual. The moments commemorated or repeated by the ritual are "re-presented," that is, made present again.

Can it be said, however, that the poet of *To Celebrate a Childhood* has accomplished what Robinson failed to do, that he has resurrected the dazzling kingdom of childhood? A dominant theme of the poem is the difference between the mythical time of childhood and time as it is experienced by the adult consciousness. To the adult mind, the lost Eden must appear as an illusion, as the result of credulousness: "In those days/a more credulous sea and haunted by invisible departures,/tiered like a sky above orchards,/was gorged with gold fruit, violet fishes, and birds" (V). The poet is no longer a child. He knows that the high condition which once was his, was only a dream: "I dreamed this, in esteem" [*"J'ai fait ce songe, dans l'estime"*] (I). *Estime* does not only mean "esteem." It is also a nautical term: "by dead reckoning." A child's vision of the world is similar to a sea journey without objective landmarks or to a dream which reflects only the subjective life of the dreamer.[7] Of this dream, nothing remains: "I dreamed this dream, it has consumed us without relics" (I). Nothing, that is, except the nostalgia. Childhood is no more, but it was a high condition. *To Celebrate a Childhood* is the commemoration of the lost kingdom, and its celebration. It is also the recognition that the magic, as much as in the world, was in the vision.

III *Praises*

Before he wrote the autobiographical poems of *To Celebrate a Childhood,* Saint-John Perse assumed a poetic mask: Robinson Crusoe. The poem "Des Villes sur trois modes" seems to occupy, in relation to *Praises,* a position similar to *Pictures for Crusoe* in relation to *To Celebrate a Childhood.* In this short work (73 lines only), the young poet assumes the mask of a pirate-captain who displays in his adventures all the violence, the lust, and the mocking contempt for organized society which make pirates and outlaws so attractive to children and adolescents. "Des Villes sur trois modes" was published in 1908, but it is dated 1906. This would indicate that it was written even before *To Celebrate a Childhood.* It thus appears that Robinson Crusoe and the pirate-captain were personae which allowed the poet to express indirectly what he did not wish to say openly. *Pictures for Crusoe* and "Des Villes sur trois modes" may therefore be considered as preparatory steps for the more frankly autobiographical *To Celebrate a Childhood* and *Praises.* "Des Villes sur trois modes" has not been collected in Saint-John Perse's *Oeuvre poétique* and cannot, for reasons of space, be discussed here.

To Celebrate a Childhood refers to the early years of childhood, when a boy is still small enough to be given a bath by his mother's maids, to be kissed by his nurse, or to cry unashamedly. Perfect bliss tends to be a passive state. In the radiant Eden of childhood, everything is given. This does not mean that all is sweet innocence, either in the child or in the world. He has experienced violence, suffering, and death. Violence also appears in the imagery but only on rare occasions: the wounding of sugar canes at the mill, the arrows of light flung forth by the sea, the spears of flame cast by the sun. Faint stirrings of sexuality may be perceived in some of the child's memories: the warm legs of tall glistening girls, or the mouth of his nurse which tasted like rose apples. The composition of *Praises* is similar to *To Celebrate a Childhood:* it is a series of eighteen short poems depicting scenes from the poet's childhood, but nostalgic celebration is no longer the dominant mood. *Praises* deals with a later stage of childhood, when sexuality and violence play a more important role in a child's psyche. The primacy of instinctive drives and the impatience with restraint expressed in "Des Villes sur trois modes" have their counterpart in *Praises,* although the Edenic ecstasy of being at one with the world remains an essential theme.

The eighteen sections of *Praises* do not seem to be arranged according to a definite scheme, although some of them appear to revolve around a central motif: sections V-IX take place at sea, X-XIV in the port town where the child went to school. Sections I-IV and XV-XVIII are more loosely connected and deal with various aspects of the child's life on the island. There is the appetizing smell of meat broiling in the open and the beauty of a horse. A man (possibly the boy's father) makes arrangements for a boat trip. A dreamer awakes. Children peek through windows to glimpse the smooth naked bodies of their nursemaids. There is a glorious morning on the island as a cool wind rises from the sea. A child hates having his hair combed and wishes to be left alone. These seemingly disconnected scenes compose a sensitive portrayal of a child's soul, unmarred by mawkish sentimentality and uncluttered by any false embellishment. They record the emotions of childhood in all their variety, ranging from wild ecstasy to total revolt or desperate resignation. They also convey a vivid representation of life on a Caribbean island at the turn of the century, especially when the liminary piece of the collection is taken into consideration.

"Written on the Door" makes an essential contribution to the understanding of *Praises,* since it gives the reader a clear indica-

tion of the social milieu where these poems originated. It also
shows that the youthful author of *Praises* realized the limitations
of the social group to which he belonged: the white plantation
owners who were the ruling class among a predominantly black
population. "Written on the Door" might be taken for such a
man's profession of faith. The word "white" recurs three times in
the poem as though to stress the theme of racial pride. The word
"black," on the other hand, is associated with creatures in a subordinate position, the "black women" or the "black hens." In this
social group, women wait at home for the master's return and see
to his comfort. The plantation owner who speaks in the poem is
proud of what he does: he works hard even when he has a bout of
fever; he rides home from the fields covered with mud; his hands
are oily from testing cocoa seeds and coffee beans. He is satisfied
with his small world and feels no yearning to go beyond its limits,
no envy for the passing ships.

The world described in *Praises* is also a closed universe, the
universe of childhood. In most of the *éloges,* the voice we hear is
that of the poet himself, of the child he once was. He speaks in the
first-person singular when he refers to himself only, in the first-
person plural when he considers himself as part of a group: his
family, his fellow passengers aboard a ship, his fellow townsmen.
In some sections, however, he appears only indirectly, as "a child,"
"the child," "the Dreamer," or "the Story-teller." The various
éloges do not appear, for the most part, as recollections of past
experiences. With one or two exceptions, the present tense is used
throughout the work, as though the scenes described were actually taking place before the poet's eyes. One section only is written entirely in the past tense (II). This change in the temporal
perspective may serve to stress the distance between the adult
consciousness of the poet and the feelings he had as a child. Similarly, as he recollects a morning at sea, he wonders: "Childhood,
my love, was it only that? . . . ," as though the magic of this
morning had passed beyond his understanding (V). Conversely,
the modification in temporal perspective may suggest a dimension
of awareness which the child still lacked. The child can say: *"mon
enfance n'a sa fin,"* but the adult knows that even then "trees were
rotting at the far end of creeks of black wine," that time brings to
a close the seemingly endless enchantment of childhood (VIII).

The first *éloge* opens abruptly, as the smell of broiling meats and brewing sauces reaches "the Dreamer with dirty cheeks" and wakes him from an "old dream all streaked with violence, wiles and radiance." The Dreamer's identity is not clearly revealed. He briefly reappears in another section, still occupied with visions of violence (XIV). The dirty cheeks, the beads of sweat which adorn him, his response to the smell of meat, the taste for violence, the lazy walk similar to that of a woman with her garments, her linen and her undone hair trailing behind her make up a significant picture. They suggest a creature whose actions are determined by its physical appetites. Physiological and biological processes are predominant. This creature shows little or no self-discipline and acts without regard for accepted rules for social behavior. The comparison with a woman points to a lack of definite masculinity. All of these details apply to a creature both fierce and tender, radiant and violent, and whose life is largely governed by instinct. Its mental activities do not appear to rise much above the level of an animal and are largely confined to daydreaming. The "Dreamer with dirty cheeks" may thus be identified as a young boy, and *Praises* as the relation of his childhood. The word "dream" (*songe*) recurs repeatedly in the work as though to express its secret essence. The world of childhood is indeed a dream in which the world also dreams: "Roadsteads dream dreams full of children's heads" (III).

In the dreamlike vision of the child, everything has a life of its own. Red bluffs appear as figures of pride while the sea is "fraudulent" (III). At the dawn of a beautiful day, the roadstead is "a prey to uneasiness" and "the sky is inspired" (XVI). A sea bird flying overhead is "wild as Cambyses and gentle as Ahasuerus" (VII). On a hot day, the city is "yellow with rancor" (XI). The sea in the morning is "rosy with lust" like a woman whose pleasure is bartered for a batch of bronze bracelets and the world itself is not "too old to burst into laughter" (XVI). The boy's animistic imagination goes far beyond the attribution of spirit, soul, and feeling to animate or inanimate objects. He establishes with them the kind of relationship which is normally restricted to human beings. The walls along which the child walks on his way home from school return his affection (XIV). He transacts business with an insect or else he has "an alliance with the blue-veined stones" (XVIII). This instinctive affinity with nature is beyond the reach of the adult. The horse he owned as a child is now a mystery:

"Who was it?" In the boy, however, there is no question about his feelings for this creature: he loves him. The horse is beautiful. Its beauty is that of life itself, and any manifestation of life, even sweat, is a thing of beauty. The following description has all the grace of an antique: "sometimes (for an animal knows better the forces that praise us)/Puffing, he would lift to his gods a head of bronze, covered with a petiole of veins" (II). It combines power ("bronze," "puffing") and delicacy ("a petiole"). But beauty is not the poet's primary concern. The horse is also a symbol of superior wisdom. Divine beings reveal themselves to him. The child is thus brought into contact with the sacred forces of life. The beast's instinct has powers which are denied to human reason. Although reason may dominate instinct as a man rides a horse, it is through his animality that man can make contact with the gods.

The mysterious forces of nature make their presence constantly felt throughout *Praises*. For a boy, a boat is a living creature. Just as a horse knows better what forces exalt us, the sail, in the strange revelation of their presence, appears as the medium of an epiphany. The gusts of wind caught by the sail are felt as the breath of a god: "O/gusts! . . . Truly I inhabit the throat of a god" (IX). The religious tone is reinforced by the vocabulary. The boat is "the Ark", and those on board seem to witness sacred rites, the "libations of the day." This is, it would appear, the true origin of Saint-John Perse's poetry. All things, under the surface, are teeming with a secret life, and this hidden life makes itself known to the daydreaming boy who is already a poet and can decipher "those tidings on a journey and those messages on the tides" (IX).

There is mention, in one of the *éloges*, of springs under the sea. During a sea journey, the youngest of the travelers offers to talk about them, and his fellow passengers beg him to tell his story. The poetry of Saint-John Perse flows from such hidden springs. It carries within itself the sacred essence of Being which reveals itself to those who retain their ties with the magic kingdom of childhood. Man cannot escape the mysterious forces which permeate every aspect of life. It almost seems that human emotions are only the product of energies which originate outside of man, in the awesome powers of nature. These powers have all the ambivalence of the Sacred. Nature reveals herself in her infinite splendor and variety. She can inspire gentleness or cruelty, tenderness or lust, joy or dread. She may recreate for the child the dream of edenic esctasy.

The milky ocean, the morning dawn, and the water on the freshly washed deck in which the sky is reflected suggest a fluid universe in which everything merges with everything. There is no separation between man and the world, no rupture within the world itself. There is only perfect harmony. The only wish left to man is to become just a thing among other things. His yearning to commune with the totality of Being can only be compared to the lover's desire to renounce his own separate individuality (V-VI). As the day progresses and grows hotter and hotter, the "adorable childhood of day" (V) yields to the "aggressive childhood of day" (VI), and, later on, to a more savage delight, "a crackling in the scarlet chasms, the abyss trampled by buffaloes of joy" (VII). As the sap which silently flows "comes out on the slender shores of the leaf", so can the wild energy of nature well up in man and erupt into sudden action. The fierceness of the noonday sun is reflected in the dream of "a sky of straw in which to hurl, O hurl! with all one's might the torch!" (XIV). The city at noon is a scene filled with mad dreams of absolute power and murderous violence.

In the fourth *éloge*, the untamed energy of nature explodes into a profusion of forms. Beasts are bursting with a cry. Crabs have devoured whole trees with their soft fruit and succulent flowers. Flies rain down as soon as one touches another tree. Ants hurry in opposite directions. Animal cries, devouring beasts, and swarming insects are typical expressions of the animal archetype which is clearly associated with sexuality.[8] The boy awakes "dreaming of the black fruit of the Aniba in its warty and truncated cupule," of "flowers in bundle under the axil of the leaves." The sexual symbolism is explicit enough. The poem is undoubtedly related to the awakening of sexual desire, but it must be pointed out that it also betrays an underlying anxiety. Animal symbols often are projections of the fears associated with sex. A whole tree has been eaten up by insects, another is covered with scars. The fear of mutilation by a devouring beast is still more apparent in the verse: "A live dog on the end of a hook is the best bait for the shark. . . ." To be sure, the fear of sexuality appears only in a disguised form. The women seen in the poem are "laughing all alone in the abutilons, the yellow-spotted-black-purple-at-the-base flowers that are used for the diarrhoea of horned animals." Through their association with the abutilons, women seem to partake of the beauty and beneficence of nature.

On the whole, the destructive powers of Nature cause neither fear nor revolt. Sometimes, men succeed in propitiating her. When oxen and mules have to be unloaded from a boat and brought to land, figurines of gods cast in gold and polished with resin are given overboard to the water. The sea responds to the ritual offering: it leaps and lifts them up (X). For the most part, the threat of Nature is accepted without question and remains a constant presence. The Cemetery reigns high over the City (XI). Earthquakes take their toll. Priests, quicklime, and solderers are available for a quick burial of the dead. The victims are carried in soldered zinc boxes by city officials along the main street. As a young boy, Saint-John Perse witnessed such funerals. He saw the dappled sky which predicted another earthquake for the evening. But if the dappled sky is an omen of death, a human figure looms as a prophet of life: "erect/and alive/and dressed in an old sack good-smelling of rice,/a Negro whose hair is black sheep's wool rises like a prophet about to shout into a conch . . ." (XII). The boy also knows the smell of rotting trees at the far end of creeks, "that avid smell of dead wood, making one think of Sun spots, astronomers, and death . . ." (VIII). But Nature's beauty is such that it can make the boy forget not only its powers of destruction, but even the splendor of legend, "the peacocks of Solomon," "the flower painted on the baldric of the Ras," or "the ocelot fed on human flesh, before the bronze gods, by Montezuma" (VIII). Similar contrasts occur in other *éloges*. A jeering fish head and a dead cat are obvious symbols of death, while the pink bitch dragging her belly of dugs and the candygirl battling the wasps are intensely alive. A coconut that has been drained and tossed away, "blind clamouring head set free from the shoulder," might tip the scales in favor of death, were it not for the triumphant appearance, on the "carnelian quay," of "a girl dressed like a Lydian king" (XIII).

IV　*The Message of Praises*

A message thus emerges. Like the child, man must submit to certain limitations. A child hates being touched, and still more having his hair combed, but he cannot escape (XVII). He may feel so frustrated that he could jump overboard: what can he do but yield (IX)? He knows the urge to rebel, to kill, and to destroy everything in sight, but all he really does is to withdraw his feet (XIV). The instinct of the child leads him to seek refuge in the companionship of nature. There is a lesson to be found in her splendor: "Meanwhile the wisdom of the day takes the shape of a fine tree/and the swaying tree,/ losing a pinch of birds,/ scales off in the lagoons of the sky a green so beautiful, there is nothing that is greener except the water-bug" (XVII). This vision combines the tree, rooted in one spot, and the pinch of birds scattered over the sky. If the tree expresses attachment to the earth, the birds suggest the conquest of space, the most complete form of freedom. Wisdom is then to be found in the balance of opposites. This may well be the message to be read in the concluding section of *Praises*. The child goes out to meet the world. He also reserves the right to withdraw within himself. Wisdom lies in the equilibrium between the world and the self, between reality and the dream. This double impulse and the resulting balance will remain fundamental features in the poetry of Saint-John Perse.

CHAPTER 2

The Glory of Man

IN the collected works of Saint-John Perse, the second cycle of poems bears the title *The Glory of Kings*. Their composition spans nearly forty years. "Recitation in Praise of a Queen" was written as early as 1907, while "Lullaby" was published only in 1945. The short poem "The Regent's Story" appeared in 1910. Both "Friendship of the Prince" and "Song of the Heir Presumptive" came out in 1924. These poems were incorporated in the first three editions of *Praises*. All of them are *éloges*, since they sing the praise of royal figures, of kings and queens, of regents and princes. There is, however, an essential difference which may explain why these poems were later gathered in a separate cycle. The object of praise is no longer the kingdom of childhood but the glory of kings. In *Praises*, man occupies only a small place in the order of things. A bird, a fish, an insect, or a stone have at least equal importance. *The Glory of Kings* stresses another fundamental theme in the poetry of Saint-John Perse: the primacy of man.

I "Recitation in Praise of a Queen"

The Queen whose praise is sung reigns over a primitive tribe of warriors. The speaker is a leader of young men, and the poem seems to be part of some ritual. This impression is reinforced by its structure, which is patterned after such liturgical forms as the psalm or the litany. In each of the five sections, the speaker addresses the Queen in praise and propitiation, and each time the chorus makes the same response: *"But who would know by what breach to enter Her heart?"* The use of a liturgical form implies no parodic intention: it merely emphasizes the sacred character of a barbaric idol. Some details in the text suggest a geographical location. The Queen's body is painted with rocou, the orange red dye which Carib Indians extracted from arnotto seeds. Reference is made to another tree indigenous to the West Indies: the sapodilla.

It is obvious, however, that the poet is not trying to recreate for his readers a tribal ceremony from pre-Columbian America. The West Indian references are purely incidental. The poem must be read in a wider context.

The Queen displays all the characteristic features of a great goddess. According to Renato Poggioli, her "magnificent fatness" is a "sign of biological vitality, of animal fecundity, of physiological warmth." [1] The abundance of her flesh has definite sexual implications. The Queen's appearance is so striking that young warriors cannot speak and mutely swallow their spittle. At the beginning of the poem, the leader of the chorus requests that they be allowed to bathe naked before their Queen. This ritual would be for them *comme un jeu sous l'huile*. In antiquity, young men oiled their bodies before taking part in athletic games. In the poem, the comparison suggests sexual playfulness and the lenitive effect of the ritual bath on the young men's "proud desire." A similar request is made again in the fourth section. The Queen is asked to spread her legs, so that the odor of her body will soothe the inflammation from which the young men suffer. The heat of sexual excitement is conveyed indirectly, although explicitly, through the imagery. The unctuous moisture of the Queen's abundant flesh is, for the young warriors, the sanctuary of their desires. They also give praise to the "splendid, tawny hair" which adorns her "hidden flank."

The Queen is for her subjects far more than an object of sexual desire: she is a superior Being, the supreme Protector of her people. She is seated. Her large body remains motionless. Her wide hands rest over her legs as powerful weights. The description is somewhat reminiscent of large seated Egyptian statues and conveys the same impression of superhuman dimensions and power, mystery and repose. A famous line from Baudelaire comes to mind—*"Je hais le mouvement qui déplace les lignes"*—although, unlike Baudelaire's Goddess of Beauty, the Queen inspires no fear. Indeed her powerful dimensions and her immobility are strangely reassuring. The essence and the source of the Queen's power are clearly indicated. The Queen is a sacred figure. The Sun and the Moon pay tribute to her sovereignty. For the speaker, she is a table of sacrifices and the table of his law. She is indeed the "Lawful One," possibly because of her magic association with the laws of Nature. She carries within herself the secret of cosmic rhythms: "the Moon that commands the tides is the same that governs, O Lawful One!/the proud rite of your menses!" (V). Men find peace in her body, but the peace she brings is not only the deliverance from the "burning memory" of sexual desire, but the deliverance from life itself: "no fruit in that infecund womb by the high navel would hang, other than,/from what secret stem,/our heads!" (III). In the young men's vision, the Queen will wear their heads as barbaric ornaments, but the prospect of decapitation brings only wild elation.

Anthropologists have noted that head-hunting and the ritual castration of enemies never coexist in the same culture. Decapitation and castration have therefore been considered as symbolic equivalents.[2] If the body of the Queen is a "table of sacrifices," the sacrifice is not dreaded, but welcomed. The destruction of the self symbolized by decapitation is experienced as erotic ecstasy. Death appears as sexual consummation. The imagery also indicates that such a death imitates the process of birth. It turns out, however, that the fruit hanging from the Queen's belly is not a live child but a head separated from a man's body. In a sense, death negates birth by repeating it in reverse. This is perhaps why the Queen's womb may be called "infecund." All life eventually leads to death. All living creatures will ultimately return to the womb which bore them, to the Mother of all things, to the enigmatic Mother Nature whose heart cannot be penetrated.

II   *"Friendship of the Prince"*

Another title for this poem might well be "Recitation in Praise of a King." Here again no reference is made to a specific location or to a definite period in history. A number of indications are given in the text, but no single area can be identified on the basis of this information. The Prince rules over a country of redlands bordered by the sea. When the wind blows from the northwest, it drives the flood tide up the rivers, deep inland. Far away, there are lands of white earth, or of slate. Only brief allusions are made to flora and fauna. There are crested birds and bats, bees and digger-wasps, marshlands and camphor woods. Figs, ipomea roots, and mimosas are also mentioned. Other details mainly serve to suggest a certain level of civilization, although they point to no particular culture. Most of these traits could be found in a great many societies at a preindustrial stage. Feudal values are very

much in evidence, as is indicated by the importance given to birth
and lineage. The kingdom has a long past. Its most ancient chronicles are preserved in books made of goatskin parchment. The
Prince likes to surround himself with learned men. His kingdom is
well governed, and his subjects seem to be proud of their social
organization. There is a feeling of superiority over men of low
civilization who wander in the mountains. Men journey mostly
because of war, or trade, or to discharge religious debts. They use
mules for traveling and chew a stimulating leaf (tobacco? coca?
betel?). When they stop to rest on their journey, they lean against
tall jars possibly used for storing and transporting grains or liquids.

The fact remains, however, that the geographical and historical
settings have but little importance in the general economy of the
poem. Its formal structure follows the same pattern as "Recitation
in Praise of a Queen." A speaker addresses the Prince and recounts his merits. Each of the four sections concludes with the
same refrain: "It is of the King that I speak, ornament of our
vigils, honour of the sage without honour." The "sage without
honour" is obviously the speaker. His only "honour" lies in the
friendship bestowed upon him by the Prince. By underlining his
own obscurity, he implies that the Prince chooses his friends not
for their high birth, but for their personal value. The speaker
never praises the Prince directly. To do so, it seems, would violate
the subtle code of etiquette which governs the relationship between a Prince "heavy with ancestors and nursling of Queens" and
a man "without honour," although a sage. By its structure and its
tone, the poem thus reminds the reader of a definite literary
genre: court poetry.

"Friendship of the Prince" purports to be the work of a wandering sage, who is also the Prince's friend and pays him periodic
visits. In the course of his journeys, he listens to what people have
to say about their King. The first two sections are presented as a
mere report of what he has heard. Many voices speak the King's
praise as the sage proceeds toward the royal residence. The third
section is made up of two letters: the Prince's welcoming message
to the visitor whose arrival has been announced, and the sage's
reply. In the final section, the sage and his convoy are greeted by
the Prince and settle for the night. This section is notable for the
abundance and precision of detail. It has all the concreteness and

evocative power of familiar scenes depicted on antique vases or bas-reliefs. We see the king seated in the shade on his threshold, between the high copper spittoons. He talks and trades jests with his companions, full of wisdom and geniality as he scratches his head under his bandanna. He takes his turn in the games played on the threshold: dice, knucklebones, marbles. To honor his guest, the Prince has donned his golden robes. He stands up and walks down several steps in order to welcome the traveler. Women put away the games; the convoy arrives; the men are lodged, bathed, and given over to the women for the night; the animals are unharnessed and cared for. Night falls. The end of the poem conveys an impression of total well-being, of perfect peace and harmony.

This atmosphere of peace and serenity is due, to all appearances, to the Prince's influence. He creates order and harmony not only in the kingdom but also in the souls of men. Everything seems to converge toward the lamp shining under his roof, which may be taken as symbolizing the victory of light over darkness, of order and harmony over madness and confusion. The Queen of "Recitation in Praise of a Queen" commands complete surrender to the elemental forces of Nature. Man ceases to exist as a distinct entity. She might be seen as a figure of the Yin principle. In "Friendship of the Prince," on the other hand, the Prince rules over the natural world: "the country is governed . . . " The Prince embodies the supremacy of the enlightened virile Spirit over dark feminine Matter, of the Yang over the Yin. His lean body and the thinness of his nostrils are but the visible expression of his spirituality. He is indeed, in every sense of the word, "subtle." The Prince thus appears at the center of a highly characterized symbolic constellation. First come the images which indicate separation, struggle, and victory. The Prince is not of this world. He stands "on the keen edge of the spirit." The cutting weapon gives him the power to separate himself from worldly concerns. He is the man apart, the nonconformist, the Dissenter. He is also divided man, a man of schisms, "at the highest point of his soul fomenting a mighty quarrel" and, "sober, seizing by its nostrils an invisible quivering beast." In this intense struggle, the spirit of man tames his own wild animal energy.

The Prince's physical appearance and his ascetic way of life give further proof of his contempt for the demands of the body. He seldom sleeps. His shining lamp expresses his refusal to yield to the influence of night. He keeps away from the demented Queen. Her madness seems to be caused by some form of hysterical nymphomania. The Prince, on the other hand, rejects "abundance on the royal couch." His austere contempt for carnality is indicated by his preference for meager mats and the thinnest girls. He purifies himself "at noon before the mouths of cisterns, casting off his fever in the hands of girls fresh as water-jars." At times, he draws a fold of cloth over his face. His "clear thoughts" are a refuge against the "monstrous putrefactions" from which he withdraws. Other details stress the theme of purity and withdrawal: the halls of quicklime which he favors, the vast naked places through which he roams at night, the bats nourished on pure figs for which he sings his most princely songs.

Another series of images carries connotations of lightness, ascent, and flight. The Prince is nourished by "the breaths of the earth," by the most insubstantial foods. He appears as light as a bird, rocking at the top of the grass, ready to take flight from this world. A third cluster of images is connected with the sacred. The Prince stands highest among men, not only because of his royal birth, but also by virtue of the dream. His aigrette is but the visible sign of his invisible election. Saint-John Perse plays upon the double meaning of the French word *huppe:* it means "crest," but it also refers to a crested bird which in antiquity was associated with Apollo, god of prophecy and poetry.[3] The Prince is indeed a *Prince par l'absurde:* his kingship has its true source in the absurd, in the mantic madness which Apollo visited upon his priestess. According to some traditions, the Pythia was, like the Prince, "obedient to the breaths of the earth" since she breathed the fumes emanating from a fissure in the rock over which she was seated. She may well have been a "great girl mad under grace rocking herself in the breath of her birth," swaying on her tripod in the ecstatic trance induced by the god.

The Prince's powers of prophecy are also suggested by his advance "through the day that has the odour of entrails." The comparison is reminiscent of the Haruspices who read the will of the gods in the entrails of sacrificial victims. The Prince thus appears as the Soothsayer. His only function among his people is "to keep vigil." He is not a man of action but of contemplation. The only battles which he wages are spiritual battles. Under the sign of his forehead, with his lashes "haunted by immortal shades," he ap-

pears as a sacred figure in communication with the supernatural.
Such is the origin of his power, the reason why sages and learned
men flock around him. The Prince is "the Healer and the Assessor
and the Enchanter at the sources of the spirit." He is also the
maker of princely songs. The Prince thus combines features of the
priest-king, the shaman, and the poet. In these capacities, he is
essentially a giver of life. In the evenings of great drought on the
earth, he is not "sterile," but "flowering on his threshold." Other
images suggest the fecundating power of his spirit. The bees
which gather around him are attracted by "his beard powdered
with a pollen of wisdom." Similarly, in the final section, "bees
leave the caverns to look for the tallest trees in the light." The
Prince is such a tall tree: "his name makes the shade of a great
tree." "Attired in his sayings," he is also "like a tree wrapped in
bands." Saint-John Perse must have been aware of the ritual and
symbolic significance of the tree and the bee in Indo-European
and Asian mythologies.[4]

One conclusion emerges: the Queen of "Recitation in Praise of a
Queen" and the King of "Friendship of the Prince" represent polar
opposites which must be interpreted in a wider context, both an-
thropological and psychological. Mythical systems are commonly
reduced to two broad categories. One is associated with the cult
of Great Goddesses, the other with the supremacy of male divinities. To all appearances, figurines representing women were the
most ancient idols of mankind. For primitive men, there was a
magic relationship between the menstrual cycle and the rhythms
of nature which control the phases of the moon, the movement of
the tides, the succession of seasons, the birth and death of vegetation. The Great Goddesses generally appear as a figure of Mother
Nature, who is both life-giving and life-destroying, forever virgin
and forever fertile, like the earth and the sea. There was no separation between man and Nature since man lived in blind submission to her power. Human sacrifices expressed the deep desire to
take part in the total cycle of cosmic creation and destruction.
Great Goddesses thus embodied man's longing to become one
with cosmic fate.

The worship of Great Goddesses must have satisfied fundamental aspirations in the human soul, since such cults have been found
in all times and in many cultures. It could be interpreted, on a

superficial level, as a yearning for the maternal womb, but a more satisfactory explanation may be suggested by a comparison with patriarchal cultures in which male Gods were objects of worship. In order to establish their supremacy over matriarchal systems, these Gods had to overcome the magic powers associated with Nature as Woman. The male Gods of Light generally triumph over female earth and sea monsters. The destructive power of the Great Goddesses was only the negative side of their power to give life, but Hellenic and Semitic mythologies tended to see only their evil aspects and turned them into monsters. The Judeo-Christian tradition preserved this distrust of the magic powers of Woman and Nature. It culminated in Augustinian puritanism, in Calvinist and Jansenist asceticism. The Good is identified with the denial of Nature, with the triumph of Spirit over Matter, of the Eternal over Time. And yet, the yearning remains for a return to the Great Mother, to the primeval unity. "Recitation in Praise of a Queen" appears as the expression of this yearning, while "Friendship of the Prince" links spiritual concerns and ascetic practices with the figure of a male hero.

This conflict could also be described, in Freudian terms, as the struggle between the id and the superego. In one case, the libido generates a kind of *amor fati* which turns men into the willing slaves of Eros-Thanatos. In the opposite case, the energy of the libido places itself under the authority of a kingly male figure, and turns the virile negativity of Thanatos against the mad feminoid Eros.[5] In "Recitation in Praise of a Queen," Saint-John Perse rediscovers the archetypal cluster of symbols in which the terror of death is euphemized through its association with the Great Mother. The poem reflects the regressive nostalgia for the dissolution of the self, the wish for the ecstatic fusion with primal Unity. "Friendship of the Prince," on the other hand, expresses man's primitive urge to master his fate through the archetypal images of the King in his triple role of Healer, Assessor, and Enchanter. He is all at once the inspired visionary, the magician with supernatural powers, the lawgiver who imposes order and stability upon the self and upon the world. Finally, on another level, the Queen and the Prince may represent the conflicting forces at work in poetry: the uncontrolled surge of inspiration and the poet's effort to subject this creative energy to the direction of his will.

III   *"The Regent's Story"*

The Queen and the Prince have the fascination of archetypes.
The societies over which they rule have not been swept up by the
current of history: they retain the fixed structure of myth. The
ruler whose figure appears in the short poem "The Regent's
Story" represents a different kind of power. His authority is not
founded on ritual, tradition or spiritual superiority. He is a "Regent," not a "King," a barbarian chief whose power has been established by brute force. The poem might well be a song of praise
recited by one of his warriors: "You conquered! You conquered!
How beautiful the blood, and the hand/that with thumb and
finger wiped off the blade!" Such a vision has indeed a savage
beauty. In the conquerors' eyes, the kingdoms they destroy deserve their fate. The scenes which have left their imprint on the
speaker's memory carry connotations of physical and moral degeneration. He recalls cripples and peaceful people, unable or unwilling to fight, and frightened women fleeing with cages of green
birds, possibly a symbol of a culture in which the soaring powers
of life have been totally subjugated. A prophet speeding on a one-
eyed camel behind the palisades may represent the cowardice, the
mutilation, and the limitation caused by a religion which the conquerors reject and despise. There remains in us enough of the
savage so that we can share in the warriors' exultation at holding
the lives of others in their power, in the wild ecstasy of yielding to
the most violent urges, in the total freedom from any restraint.

The warriors' fascination with death is powerfully expressed in
the final scene which describes a strange ritual. Funeral pyres are
loaded with "human fruit" and the dead are cremated to the
music of flutes and triangles. The bones are then gathered and
preserved in pure wine. Critics have speculated about the poet's
sources: was he influenced by Byzantine chronicles? Did he have
in mind the exploits of Timur or other conquerors? [6] Saint-John
Perse, a distinguished classicist, might have read of a similar ritual
in the *Odyssey* (canto XXIV) and in the *Aeneid* (Book VII, 212-
35). I am also inclined to relate this poem to Mallarmé's contempt
for the "human fruit" or to Valéry's yearning for *je ne sais quelle
sévère essence*. The trophies preserved in pure wine are white
bones. The Kings who lie naked in the odor of death accomplish

man's ultimate destiny. Fire consumes the corruptible flesh. What remains can challenge the destructive power of time.

IV *"Song of the Heir Presumptive"*

As "The Regent's Story," the "Song of the Heir Presumptive" expresses dissatisfaction with stagnation and decay. The speaker's first command implies his rejection of the past: "Draw into the shade, on his threshold, the old man's painted chair." The young heir-apparent, on the other hand, appears as the promise of the future. Each of the three stanzas begins with the same affirmation —"I honour the living"—as the speaker rejoices at finding himself surrounded by men full of life and ready for adventure. Women are ordered to nourish on earth the "thin thread of smoke" which apparently symbolizes the human presence on earth. The smoke rising at the end of promontories would then suggest the conquering urge of man to reach all frontiers. In the last stanza, as the speaker makes ready to depart, the imagery turns the universe into a domain peopled with tame creatures ready to welcome their master. In "The Regent's Story," the destruction of ancient kingdoms leads to a new purity. In the "Song of the Heir Presumptive," a dying past ("the house heavy with honours and the year yellow among the leaves") must be rejected so that the paths of the world will open before man.

V *"Lullaby"*

The final poem in *The Glory of Kings* emphasizes a similar theme: the deadliness of the past. The title is ironical, since the poem is actually a funeral lament for the firstborn child of a royal family. Since it was a girl, her birth was a bad omen, a breach in the cosmic order, and a cause of trouble for the entire kingdom: the priests, the people, the gods, the diplomats, the astronomers. The child was a mistake which had to be corrected. Instead of a queen's milk, she was fed the poisonous milk of euphorbia. She was embalmed, washed with gold, and laid to rest in a tomb among black stones. Only a donkey-man wept over her, only an old woman loved her, a very old woman soon fated to die. The King gives orders: "Let the chamber be painted a bright colour/ And the male flower on the brow of the Queens. . . ." Sons will be born; order is restored: the innocent victim is forgotten.

The poem contains an impressive number of references to specific cultural features: the importance of astrology, the ritual mur-
der of children born under unfavorable auspices, the significance
of male issue, the use of euphorbia sap for poison, the burial customs, the rites favoring the conceiving of a male child. Honey and
millet are common foods. Rocking chairs are made of rattan.
There are goatskins for carrying water. Donkeys serve as beasts of
burden. Scribes use clay cylinders for bookkeeping. Agaves are
indigenous plants. Crickets are used as pets, and the song of
orioles is heard in the land. With so much to go on, any trained
anthropologist could easily make a definite identification: it appears, however, that no civilization combines all of these traits.
Saint-John Perse seems to have borrowed from a variety of cultures. Several details are Chinese; others are reminiscent of India
(women who paint a sign on their forehead) or Assyria (the use
of clay cylinders for bookkeeping). Heterogeneous details have
been joined together with such art that an imaginary civilization
comes to exist for the reader.

The poem is in many ways reminiscent of a folk ballad, first of
all, by its form. With the exception of "Des Villes sur trois modes,"
it is the only poem written by Saint-John Perse in a single meter,
the octosyllable. It has eleven five-line stanzas. There are, however, significant departures from the conventional rules of French
versification. The lines are unrhymed, and the octosyllabic rhythm
is preserved, in many cases, by allowing an unaccented *e* to remain silent: "*Se tais[ent] les femmes aux cuisines . . . ; Gênait
les gens de chancel[le]rie. . . .*" This carefree treatment of
rhyme and rhythm is common practice in folk poetry. By the subject and by the tone, "Lullaby" could also be compared to such
funeral laments as *Le Roi Renaud* or *Lord Randal.* It recounts a
pathetic event, but the tone remains strangely detached. An innocent child may be the victim of the traditional order of things.
There is no drama and no revolt. The poem merely states what is:
an infant child must die if her birth contradicts the astrologer's
calculations.

"Lullaby" was written during World War II. It is intriguing to
note that Malraux, in *Les Noyers de l'Altenburg,* also written at
that time, takes up a similar theme. One of the characters, the
ethnographer Möllberg, describes an archaic civilization in which
every single aspect of life was commanded by the movement of

the stars. Children born on moonless days were killed at birth. The King and Queen were strangled if an eclipse of the moon occurred when the planet Venus, instead of appearing in the evening, rose in the morning. This civilization lived in the realm of absolute fatality. Another character in the novel, Vincent Berger, recognizes that man has no power over his fate: he did not choose to be born; he will not choose to die; he did not select his parents; he has no power over time. Berger must admit that the world is not what man would have made it if he had been its creator. In this perspective, art appears as a correction of the world, as a means of escaping man's fate. Berger then makes an all-important observation about Greek tragedy: many believe that representing a fatality is tantamount to being its victim. The opposite is true. Representing it, conceptualizing it, makes this fatality into something else. It no longer exists above man, in the pitiless realm of the gods: it is reduced to a human scale.[8] In "Lullaby," a voice is raised in song over the death of a child. Its detachment is only an appearance. A single song challenges the primeval order of blind human subservience to the movement of the stars. It does not seem unreasonable to see in this poem a poignant defense of naked life against the "superior" claims of historical Necessity.

VI *Thematic Unity in The Glory of Kings*

Although the poems of *The Glory of Kings* were written at different times, the fact that they were brought together in a single cycle should not be underestimated. Their juxtaposition gives them an added meaning. *The Glory of Kings* illustrates the power of man to create these highest expressions of himself: civilizations. Each poem suggests a different pattern of culture, and each pattern reflects a different system of values. It is clear, nevertheless, that each civilization is only the ultimate product of a deep human aspiration. Men have yearned for the ecstatic surrender of their individual consciousness. They have dreamed of a world subordinated to spiritual power. They have chosen the violence of war as an expression of their heroic defiance of death and rejected the ways of the past to follow the smoke of the dream. They have sung of the tears shed over one dead child and thereby shaken the foundations of the ancestral order. *The Glory of Kings* sings the glory of man.

CHAPTER 3

The Human Anabasis

FROM 1916 to 1921, Alexis Leger served as a member of the French Legation in Peking. In the Western hills, at one day's ride from the capital, he rented a disused Taoist temple which overlooked the caravan routes to the Northwest. *Anabasis* is reported to have been written there. Its publication, in 1924, brought instant critical fame to the author, at least among his peers.

I The Narrative Structure of Anabasis

Anabasis is generally considered as a narrative poem. It is divided into ten cantos. There are, in addition, one opening and one closing song. Most critics assume that the protagonist who says *I* is a single individual, although it has been suggested that there may be several characters who speak in turn.[1] It is, however, impossible to know with absolute certainty who the speaker is at any given time. I am inclined to consider the poem as a chorus of several voices which give expression to man's conflicting aspirations. At a time when Greek was still an essential part of a boy's education, the title must have reminded French readers of their school years, since Xenophon's *Anabasis* was used as a textbook in every French *lycée*. In his *Kurou Anabasis,* Xenophon describes the expedition led by Cyrus against his brother Artaxerxes, king of Persia. Saint-John Perse's poem is actually more reminiscent of Arrian's *Anabasis,* which relates Alexander's Asian campaigns. The place-names mentioned in the poem recall regions or cities conquered by Alexander's army. There are also allusions to events which occurred in the course of Alexander's conquests: the foundation of cities, the distribution of conquered territories, the use of marriage for political ends, the urge to reach the extremity of the earth, and to customs prevalent in the Asian countries traversed by his armies.[2] These similarities, however, remain rather superficial.

Since time immemorial, nomadic tribes have left their Asian homelands and marched toward the west. The expedition described in *Anabasis* appears as a legendary reconstruction of such a migration, while the protagonist is a composite portrait of the men who led nomadic horsemen to the western lands where new civilizations would evolve in all their multifarious diversity. The action of *Anabasis* cannot be placed in any definite cultural, geographical, or historical setting. The poem transcends history. It takes on the appearance of an ancient literary monument, mutilated and rhapsodic. Confronting *Anabasis,* the reader must feel as though he were reading the sacred books or the primitive epics of ancient civilizations. He is puzzled by allusions to unknown rites, to forgotten beliefs and customs. The poem was written in our days, but it seems to come to us from the depths of time, from a mythical antiquity which draws upon many archaic civilizations.[3] In spite of this fragmentary, mosaiclike character, most critics see the poem as a self-sufficient narrative structure, although there is little agreement on its meaning. It is impossible, within the scope of this study, to discuss the various interpretations which have been proposed. The mere fact of their existence gives an indication of the difficulties encountered by Saint-John Perse's readers.[4] It also testifies to the evocative power of his poetry.

II *Opening Song*

As the poem begins, an unidentified Speaker relates the foaling of a colt under a bronze tree. A passing Stranger has placed bitter berries in the Speaker's hands, and there is talk of other lands. The first stanza ends with a salute: "Hail, daughter! under the most considerable of the trees of the year." The various elements presented here suggest conflicting forces within the human soul. If the bronze tree expresses greatness, sovereignty, maturation, and the majesty of established order, it also suggests immobility, rigidity, and lifelessness. The birth of the colt, on the other hand, is associated with the emergence of life. It suggests the animal force which, since primeval times, carried man forward. Variations of the salute recur at the end of the second and the third stanzas: "My Soul, great girl, you have your ways which are not ours"; "Hail, daughter! robed in the loveliest robe of the year." There is a play upon the double meaning, in French, of the word *fille,* "daughter" and "girl." There may also be an echo, in the salute, of the Angel's words to the Virgin Mary. *Je vous salue, Marie* (Hail Mary) sounds very much like *Je vous salue, ma fille.* The reader has no sure way of knowing by whom the three salutes are spoken: by the first Speaker? by the passing Stranger? or first by one and then by the other? I believe they should be attributed to the Speaker, and that they suggest the inner changes caused by the Stranger's words. The Speaker's soul is identified with a feminine creature ready to follow the divine messenger.

The second stanza brings further precisions. The sun is entering the sign of Leo. It stands therefore exactly in the middle of the dog-days, at the peak of its power. The Stranger has placed his finger in the mouths of dead men. He laughs. The gesture is structurally equated to the placing of bitter berries in the Speaker's hands. The Stranger thus appears as a bearer of life among the dead. His laughter is a challenge to death and possibly to the deadening rule of the sun. The tidings which he brings of an herb are fascinating news to the Speaker who marvels over the *souffles* in the provinces mentioned by the Stranger. The word *souffles,* with its dual meaning of "breath" and "breeze," endows these faraway lands with the very spirit of life. A feeling of excitement is conveyed by the metaphors of easy ways, of a trumpet call, of a soaring wing. The second salute to the daughter-soul may be interpreted as the recognition, by the Speaker, that his soul is no longer his. It has received from the Stranger the bitter seeds of an aspiration which will not be denied. It no longer owes its primary loyalty to the large tree under which it first flourished, to the crowning achievement rooted in the depths of the past. The trumpet call is also the call to action, and the "feather adept of the scandal of the wing" probably refers to the glory of life striving for new heights, although it may also suggest the art of the poet who will celebrate this glory.

In the third stanza, the birth of the colt, the gift of the berries and the passing of the Stranger result in a great noise in the bronze tree. Its silent rigid mass has received the breath of life. A similar conflict between life and death may be found in the expression "Roses and bitumen, gift of song." Bitumen, which was used for embalming, is connected with death, and *les roses de la vie* are a common symbol for the ephemeral glory of life. The song is born of this struggle. The following exclamation, "Thunder and fluting in the rooms," suggests the opposition of natural forces and cosmic space to the soft music and narrow confines of human dwellings. In the final salute, the Speaker has perhaps come to realize that his soul has never been more beautiful than since it listened to the Stranger's call. Most of the elements introduced in the opening Song reappear in the ten cantos of the poem, although not necessarily with the same connotations in each occurrence. This is an essential feature of the poet's art: the modulation of basic symbols, such as the figures of the Stranger, the girl or the horse.

III   Canto I. Conflict of Past and Future

Like the opening Song, the first canto is divided into three parts. Here again, the forces of order and stability conflict with the urge of life to move forward. In the first part, the Speaker appears as a nomadic Leader intent on preserving the integrity of his law. The bright weapons, the virgin land, the incorruptible sky, and especially the sun are the symbols of this law. It would appear, however, that its power has become sterile. Life is change, and the sun opposes change. The sea, possibly because it represents an invitation to departure, is considered as "a presumption of the mind." An invocation follows: "Power, you sang as we march in darkness. . . . At the pure ides of day what know we of our dream, older than ourselves?" There is, however, no sure indication that the power which sang on the nocturnal roads may still be identified with the sun. In the pure light of morning, what do men know of the dream which preceded? A conquest has been made. Light has succeeded darkness. In the triumph of its first achievements, a civilization may forget its dark origins. The Speaker promises to remain for one more year among his nomadic followers. He will not call to the occupants of another shore, nor will he become a builder of cities. He will stay among the tent-dwellers: "Yet one more year among you! Master of the Grain, Master of the Salt, and the commonwealth on an even beam!" If grain is for the body, salt is for the spirit. The even beam indicates that equity and justice are ensured, that an even balance is maintained between physical and spiritual con-

cerns. For the time being, the nomadic horde appears as the repository of the "idea," of the creative energy of life. Glory,
strength, spiritual power, judicial authority, purity, and stability
are significantly associated with salt and light.

A different theme emerges in the second part. The voice heard
by the Speaker brings another message and his soul burns with a
pure flame, "invisible and insistent as a fire of thorns in the gale."
He stands among his people as the living expression of their unconscious aspirations. The dreams of men cannot be reduced to a
single form. Men may live in tents and dream of a city. The cosmic force of life, the wind, fans the flame of the soul. The song of
power is heard again, but the nocturnal roads are now "splendid
roads." A promise is made: "In the delight of salt the mind shakes
its tumult of spears. . . . With salt shall I revive the dead mouths
of desire!" Salt is no longer associated with the stability of past
achievements but with spiritual yearning. Its action is similar to
that of the Stranger in the opening Song: it causes life to return
among the dead. Salt causes thirst, thirst is a form of desire, and
desire leads to conquering action. The sun and its power are still
mentioned, but only in parentheses, possibly to indicate their
weakening influence. Salt, on the other hand, is the sign of men
who have a single thing in common: the urge to go elsewhere.
These are men of the frontier. The salt of their desire is never
stronger than when "at morning with omen of kingdoms and
omen of dead waters swung high over the smokes of the world,
the drums of exile waken on the marches/Eternity yawning on
the sands." New lands are only a pretext for departure. The real
motive is the wish to pursue the seeds and the breaths of life beyond the limits of the known, to march through eternity, to reach
the very end of time.

In the third section, a promise is repeated: "For another year
among you." But the Speaker is already listening to another call.
He appears divided between two equally powerful forces: the
fidelity to past conquests and the lure of the sea. The "breath" or
"breeze" of life which is the promised destiny of his people is to be
found on other shores. The fate of the future hangs in the balance.
If the seeds of time are to bear their fruit, the scales must be
tipped forward toward the brilliance of a new age. The conclusion
of the canto suggests the tension between the exquisite equilibrium of a civilization at its peak and the forward pull of history.

The "calculations hung on the floes of salt" or the "idea pure as salt" holding "its assize in the light time" may express the spiritual achievement of the race, the ideal balance reached by a given culture; they also suggest the frozen perfection of immobility. The poem of mankind, on the other hand, is the rapturous song of a race departing for its expedition on the seas of a never-ending future.

IV Canto II. The Obstacles of Sex and Death

In the first canto, the call of the future had to overcome the attachment to a frozen way of life. In the second canto, other obstacles must be faced. The Speaker and his followers are walking in a land of high slopes where the linen of the Great is spread to dry. They step over the lace dress of the Queen: it is stained at the armpit. They step over the lace dress of her daughter: a lizard catches ants at the armpit. In the space of a single day, a man may lust for a woman and her daughter. Thus, women seem to place traps in the way of men. Woman and sex are associated with impurity and animality, with a devouring beast and its powerless victims, with fornication and incest. The hour is noon. In the Bible, this is the time when evil stalks its prey. The power of the sun is once again associated with the arrest of time, with evil and death. In the opening Song, the Stranger could put his finger in the mouths of the dead and laugh. Now the dead are laughing: "Knowing laugh of the dead, let this fruit be peeled for us." Such is the ironic lesson taught by the forever grinning skulls. If the true goal of man is death, the only solace left to mortal man is to be found in immediate sensual gratification, in the perishable fruits of the earth.

The following verse seems to cry out against the hedonism of despair: "How, under the wild rose is there no more grace to the world?" Is there truly no joy waiting for man in the wilderness? Can the knowledge of death rob mortal man of any higher purpose, of all motive for action? This could be the evil mentioned in the verse: "Comes from this side of the world a great purple doom on the waters." The gathering clouds which forecast a storm appear as a *grand mal violet*, as a purplish abscess, as a threat of infection and death. A sudden gust of wind scatters the drying wash "like a priest torn in pieces." The wind blowing from the sea restores life and dispels the morbid spell. The feelings of guilt and fear com-

monly associated with sex and death are also commonly connected with the notion of sin. Once again, the wind is the cosmic
force which disperses, not only the obstacles to action raised by
the lures of the flesh and the awareness of death, but also the
paralyzing doubts fostered by religious scruple. The conquering
principle asserted in the first canto triumphs over the temptation
of Woman, the stultifying obsession with Death, and the stifling
power of Morality.

V   *Canto III. Defiant Affirmation of Life*

The third canto begins with these simple words: "Man goes out
at barley harvest." The results of past efforts have been gathered.
Man is no longer a tent-dweller, a nomadic horseman. He has a
roof over his head and he tills the land, but he proves unwilling to
remain within the protective confines of his walls. He answers the
strong voice which spoke above his roof and which will be
echoed, in Canto VI, by the call of the wind in the West. Kings sit
at his doorsteps and the Ambassador eats at their table. These
personages may also be considered as messengers from faraway
lands, as figures of the Stranger. The Assayer of Weights and
Measures is apparently pursuing an inspection trip. Borne by the
"imposing rivers," he carries with him all sorts of debris, dead
insects, and bits of straw. The Assayer of Weights and Measures
suggests the power of the "idea," the conquering urge of a given
civilization to bring the whole world under the rigid control of its
law. He rides high on the crest of history, but he takes with him
only lifeless remains. No civilization can force its pattern upon
the future. This may be why the Speaker, who is man himself
(*l'homme*), now openly challenges the power of the sun.

The sun is accused of telling lies, of fomenting dissension, of
causing scandal. Readers may recall Rostand's famous "Hymn to
the Sun" ("Were it not for you, O Sun,/Things would be only
what they are"), Valéry's *"Ebauche d'un Serpent"* where the sun
is the devil's accomplice and causes delusion, or Plato's myth of
the cave. It is not easy, at this point, to determine the crimes of
which the sun stands accused. The Speaker's heart twitters with
joy under the dazzling splendor of whitewashed walls and the
bird sings: *"ô vieillesse!"* ("O Senectus!"). The word is an echo
of *"notre aînesse"* in the first canto ("our dream, older than
ourselves"). The human heart is thus likened to a bird and to

the dream which sang on the nocturnal roads. For men in whom the dream sings its perennial song, the rivers of time do not run dry. They are to be taken as a man takes a woman. The poet's vision of human history is expressed in highly concentrated imagery: "Ha! ampler the story of the leaf shadows on our walls, and the water more pure than in any dream, thanks thanks be given it for being no dream!" The poet's imagination creates a significant link between the leaves (which recall the tree and periodic renewal), the shadows which they project (which are also the events making up the history of man), and the water (which represents the flow of time). Man may be mortal, but his life is not a dream. And yet, the Speaker's soul is full of untruth, presumably under the influence of the sun. A powerful smell overcomes him and a doubt arises about the reality of things. But he is determined not to yield to melancholy: if a man finds pleasure in his sadness, let him be put to death. There is, later in the canto, a man who finds pleasure in the smell of burning excrement. The enjoyment of sadness, the melancholy meditation on the transience of things thus appear as a form of perversion, as a seed of corruption which must be uprooted before it spreads.

The sun is again accused of mendacity: it will be treated as Xerxes once punished the rebellious seas. The guilt of the sun may now be ascertained. The sun is any Absolute which would persuade man that the only reality is that of the "law," of the "pure idea." It would turn the history of man into a mere shadow by reducing it to what Yeats might call "a spume that plays/Upon a ghostly paradigm of things." [5] No "law," no "idea" must be allowed to take precedence over the inebriating enthusiasm of human passion. The wild heart of man must reject such a message, since the vastness of space (or the infinity of time) presents no limit to his conquering desire.

The power of the sun has been rejected; the power of signs and dreams returns in the person of "such an one, son of such an one, a poor man." Such men will guide the destiny of mankind and open the roads of the future. They will be princes, ministers, captains with stentorian voices, doers of great things, and seers of dreams. They leave behind them a doomed culture: puritanical priests proposing laws against depraved women; disputes on points of grammar held in the open; a tailor hanging new clothes made of fine velvet on an old tree; a man sick with gonorrhea washing his

linen in pure water; and the oarsman on his bench enjoying the
smell of the weakling's burning stool. All these scenes suggest
bestiality, sophistry, sumptuary excesses, sickness, pollution,
pleasure in corruption, and sterility.

The conclusion of the canto brings together a number of themes
previously introduced separately. The time is "the longest day of
the bald year," the summer solstice. As in the opening Song, this
season is associated with sterility and death. The Speaker senses a
powerful presence behind him, following in his footsteps and
praising the earth under the grass. In the opening Song, the
Stranger also spoke of the grass growing in other lands. The mysterious presence thus asserts the principle of life, of renewal in the
face of death. Several sentences of the canto are also repeated at
the beginning of the final section: "Man goes out at barley harvest. The strong smells encompass me, and the water more pure
than that of Jabal makes sound of another age. . . ." In the Bible,
Jabal is the father of such as dwell in tents and of such as have
cattle (Gen. 4:20). The word also means, in Hebrew, the current
of a river and carries connotations of exultation. Finally, Jabal is
the name of a province in ancient Persia.[6] The name may therefore suggest a legendary past, possibly the mythical origin of the
race. It may also express the attraction of a faraway land, the
belief in a triumphant future. When the grain has been harvested,
man is no longer tied to the land. Once again, he is free to face the
mystery of his destiny. The dead, under the sand, the urine and
the salt of the earth, are like chaff when the grain has been given
to the birds. They can be treated like empty husks. The living
must not be the slaves of a dead past. In the first canto, the delight of salt and the desert sands are linked to man's conquering
desire. The allusion to urine may be related to the conclusion of
canto IX, where it also appears as a defiant assertion of life.

At the end of canto III, the Speaker's soul stands watch noisily
at the gates of death. The noise it makes is a manifestation of the
wild energy of life confronting the limits set by time. The conclusion of the canto brings a resolution to the conflict. A noisy Prince
is silenced while a horse's skull is raised high on a lance. The noisy
Prince recalls the noisy soul at the gates of death. If the horse
symbolizes the animal force of life which carries man forward
through the deserts of space and time, the dead skull could signify
the loss of this force. The gesture which raises it high on a lance

may then be interpreted as man's affirmation of life against death, negation, and despair.

VI *Canto IV. Founding of the City*

This canto provides another illustration of the struggle between man's desire to design a pattern for life and his refusal to remain attached to any fixed form. This conflict is accepted as necessary and good. In the long march of mankind, the City (or any other pattern of culture) can be only a temporary stopping place. The first verses of the canto convey the exhilaration which accompanies the creative stage of a new civilization, the sense of power which comes to man when he changes the face of the earth, when he clears virgin land and secures a water supply. The "operations of channelling the living waters" also create a symbolic link between the builders of the City and the continuous flow of history. They seem to tap the energy of life itself. At the dawn of a new civilization, the world reveals itself to man with a new freshness, just as it did to the nomadic Leader. New and complex uses are found for man's creative energy.

And yet, amidst the hustle and bustle of the new City, indications already point to the threat of stagnation, death, and corruption. Incoming ships, after negotiating the bar, stop in "that dead water where floats a dead ass." The pale river is also associated with stagnation and death: it has no future (*sans destin*), and its color is that of "grasshoppers squashed in their sap." Trash accumulates in "this quarter of vacant lots and rubbish." A child, "sorrowful as the death of apes," offers a quail in a pink slipper: he is actually soliciting for his sister. There is, mostly, the sense that something has been lost. The peace and beauty of nature, her promise and her fruits will soon be stifled by culture, represented here by the vulgar ugliness of urban life. There will be festivities, shouting, and election speeches. There will be a yellow city, with girls' underwear hung out to dry in the windows. At dawn, sanitation workers will clear away large dead palms, "fragments of giant wings." The image suggests an interrupted flight, the corruption and death of the dream.

At the end of the canto, a brief separate section describes a new departure. Three moons have gone by, which echo the "three great seasons" of the first canto and may suggest the accelerated pace of historical change. The men who watched on the hillcrests

fold their tents: they have refused to become the prisoners of the
City. The body of a woman is burnt in the sands, possibly to
express contempt for the carnal indulgence associated with the
City, or because woman represents stability, the refusal to go
forth toward the unknown. A man advances toward the desert,
the son of a flask-maker. In the desert, containers for liquids are a
basic necessity.[7] Those who depart seek for new waters. They are
resuming the quest for the amniotic fluid associated with the regeneration of time, with the continuous flow of life.

VII   Canto V. New Dreams of Departure

The conflict within the Speaker's soul now takes the form of a
struggle between his followers and the contradictory aspirations
of his soul. A contrast is indicated between the towns with their
"hundred fires revived by the barking of dogs," which suggest a
domesticated way of life, and the "fire of thorns in the gale" mentioned in the first canto. The Speaker's extravagant supporters are
delighted with his achievements, but his thoughts are already
elsewhere. A question is asked: "Leader of a people of dreams to
be led to the Dead Seas, where shall I find the water of night that
shall bathe our eyes?" Which images of man will the Speaker lead
to the shores of the Dead Seas? In the dark night of his soul, can
his eyes be cleansed and see clearly? The answer is that vision can
be conquered only through conflict, and this struggle is translated
into external symbols. Companies of stars pass on the edge of the
world, so that a kitchen fire seems to become one of their number.
Later in the canto, a star is said to have been surprised by night in
the servant-girls' quarters. This symbolic link between the night-
star and the figure of woman recurs in cantos IX and X. If the star
may be considered as a symbol of the Divine, this detail may suggest that the cult of Woman could become a goal for man's aspirations.

This cult, however, conflicts with other forms of transcendence.
Over the Speaker's roof, the Confederate Kings of Heaven are
conducting a war and have established their quarters in the
heights. It is the Speaker's wish to join the breaths of night,
among the "pamphleteering Princes," among the falling meteors.
The Speaker seems to express man's primeval desire to secede
from the earth, to become one with the gods, to share in the action
of cosmic forces. In the solitude of night, the soul experiences an-

other temptation: it yearns for silent communion with the Dead Women. To the lips of the prodigal son, the night gives milk and honey. After the wish to conquer transcendence comes the wish to return to the Woman of Saba, to the Dark Mother, to primeval Night. The Confederate Kings of Heaven and the Dark Woman thus seem to be related to the two fundamental aspirations of the human imagination. One is associated with virility, sovereignty, military power, elevation, and light. The other combines images of femininity, the giving of food, death, and night. Both are, however, the nocturnal temptations of dream, and the Speaker rises against them. He will depart with the wild geese, in the stale smell of morning. As he does so, he betrays "the least sober soul," he is still "roused from the pure pestilences of night." The nocturnal activity of the dream is a form of intoxication, of disease. Action is incompatible with the dream, although it is related to it: it is the extension, or the actualization, within the realm of concrete reality, of the visions of the night. In his adventure, the Speaker does indeed fluctuate between conquering action and the renunciation of all action.

Meanwhile, in the desert, new spears were already pursuing the "silicates of Summer," the powerful salts of desire. Dawn brings its message. The shores of the Dead Seas have been reached and its waters used for bathing. Possibly as a result of this contact with death, with the arrest of time, "those who lay naked in the enormous season" arise in crowds and proclaim the insanity of this world. It must be recalled that the people to be led to the Dead Seas is *un peuple d'images*. If the analogy is justified, the insanity of the world is illustrated by these images themselves: the old man blinking his eyes in the yellow light, the woman stretching her bones, the colt nuzzling its chin in the hand of a child who will soon dream of putting out the animal's eye. The Stranger who reappears at the end of the canto may then be viewed as the embodiment of man's rebellion against the limits of his own humanity: "there is no more substance of man in him." The concluding sentence could then be read as a general comment: "And the earth in its winged seeds, like a poet in his thoughts, travels. . . ." Man's grandeur lies in his refusal of human limitations. The winged words of the poets are identified with the winged seeds of the earth: both are manifestations of telluric energies, of the cosmic power of generation by which life propagates itself through

space and time and perpetuates itself through all crises and meta-
morphoses. The Stranger is no longer a mere human being; he is
the very essence of life which transcends all.

VIII   *Canto VI. The Traps of Happiness*

The conflict between man's wish to enjoy the fruits of the earth
and his urge to go beyond the limits of human action is again the
central theme of this canto. The Speaker and his followers are
now powerful military governors. Their power and their wealth
have enabled them to set "springes for happiness." They had believed that comfort and luxury would mean felicity, that perfumed girls in transparent dresses, the sound of ice in their drinks,
golden plates, and servant-girls would dispel the boredom of the
desert sands at the limits of the world. And then the winds came.
Here again, sedentary men hear over their roof the call to adventure. Horsemen at the end of capes publish their deeds over the
seas: "a fiery bulletin," "a history for men, a song of strength for
men, like a shudder of space shaking an iron tree." Man's insatiable need to go further takes again the symbolic form of military
conquest.

As he has done before, the Speaker voices his contempt for those
who have not tasted the fiery pleasure of action. He proclaims the
joy of "causing at the borders exceptional accidents," of going to
the extreme limits of human strength. There are men who respond
to the strong Leader who will squander and devour their strength
as a grape on the vine. They will follow the Master who believes
in his fortune and who tempts them with the role of empire-
builders which they hope to play on the stage of history or with
the promise of wealth and comfort. The dream of conquest thus
closes upon itself. The would-be conquerors are merely repeating
their previous adventure. What they now visualize in the mirror
of their dreams is the sea which rusts the swords and the return,
one evening, to the maritime provinces, to their land of leisure
and to their perfumed girls. Destiny calls on their threshold.
There is for them, in the West, "a widowhood of laurels." The
laurels of glory, when the sun sets in the West, are like women
deprived of men. In this canto, their call is not answered. In the
hands of young girls, a smell of violets and clay intrudes upon the
dreams of conquest. The winds are quieted and take shelter in
the hollow of desert gulfs. Women, flowers, and clay appear again

as reminders of mortality and still the yearning for action by revealing its apparent vanity.

IX *Canto VII. Confrontation with Death and Oblivion*

The basic conflict of *Anabasis* is presented once more in the opening verse: "We shall not dwell forever in these yellow lands, our pleasance. . . ." Man becomes aware of his transiency, in space and in time, while the expanse of the earth appears before his eyes with the color of "immortal things." In this sterile landscape of micaceous stones, man feels concern for the fate of life: the only living creatures, in the sunlit silence, are a family of crickets. The entire landscape seems to be marching slowly and silently toward the place where nations vanish in "the dead powder of the earth." The dust clouds rising up in smoke above dry riverbeds suggest the fate meted out to entire centuries of human history. Once again, the thought of death leads the Speaker to ask: can such gentleness in the heart of man fail to find satisfaction? He is addressing his soul, all "darkened by the horse smell," by the intoxicating energy which enables man to proceed in its endless march. All around him are prophetic signs urging him forward. Large birds navigating in the West recall the sea birds of canto IV. In the East, the sky is pale, "like a holy place sealed by the blind man's linen." A storm is brewing, and the clouds take on the appearance of cancerous growths. Holiness, blindness, and disease are strangely associated with the East: man must turn away from his past, from the place of his origin, lest he become its victim. The clouds which a breeze can blow out of reach are the image of his past glories. Man must turn toward the marvels which the earth can bring forth.

At noon, as a tree bursts open the stones of monuments to the dead, man closes his eyes and communes with the past. Dreaming of the marches which ended in dusty oblivion, of the empty roads traveled by forgotten predecessors, he wonders: "where find, where find the warriors who shall watch the streams in their nuptials?" How can he be sure that the rivers of time will not run dry, that there will be warriors to fecundate them? But man cannot accept the answer of despair: "At the sound of great waters on march over the earth, all the salt of the earth shudders in dream." Suddenly voices are heard. They proclaim man's revolt against death and oblivion. If rivers must die and warriors are no more, let monuments of stone and bronze take their place: "Levy a wilderness of mirrors on the boneyards of streams, let them appeal in the course of ages! Erect stones to my fame, erect stones to silence; and to guard these places, cavalcades of green bronze on the great causeways! . . ." These monuments are mirrors of man. They reflect images of himself which can sustain him when he faces annihilation. In the concluding verse, the shadow of a large bird crosses the Speaker's face as a favorable omen for his abiding faith in the future of life.

X   Canto VIII. The Long March Resumes

The long march has started again. The dominant color is not, as in the preceding canto, that of "immortal things," but the "man colour." The expedition has symbolic companions. Waterspouts, compared to clepsydras traveling over the earth, recall the "great waters on march over the earth," the continuity of human history. The "solemn rains" contain a marvelous substance, powders and insects. For the men who have answered the call of the wilderness, like the Hebrews who followed Moses, the earth fulfills its promise and brings forth marvels: "To the scale of our hearts was such vacance completed!" Only the empty expanse of the desert could be equal to their hearts' desire. This emptiness is not, however, the wasteland of solitary dreams. The march through the desert is not sterile, although the expedition does not seek material wealth or power. These men expand the frontiers of the human spirit. They wage war against spiritual darkness. The violence of their action will compel the earth to yield its secrets. They have another enemy: "These shadows—the prevarications of sky against the earth." Their struggle pits them against the mystery of the supernatural, of the Sacred. The horsemen ride through nations divided by hatred: will they raise their whips over the "gelded words of happiness," over the sterile promise of well-being and plenty? A command is given: "Man, weigh your weight measured in wheat. A country here, not mine. What has the world given me but this swaying of grass? . . ." It is beneath contempt to equate human worth and material goods. These words also express a nomad's scorn for a sedentary way of life, for the tiller of the land and the fruits of his labor. The Speaker appears as an eternal wanderer on the face of the earth. The only gift which he will acknowledge is the motion of the grass, the visible trace of an invisible progress: the winds of life blowing across the earth.

The expedition finally reaches the Dry Tree, in ancient times, the end of the known world. Alexander's purpose, when he set the Ganges as his goal, was to march to what he considered to be the extremity of the earth. In the economy of *Anabasis*, where the march through space appears as a symbol of the human march through time, the Dry Tree may be considered as the limit between man's past and his future. It indicates the point when man may cease to exist, the moment in time when the human species may vanish into nothingness. But the Dry Tree was also, according to legend, the tree of Abram which would again grow green after centuries of apparent death.[9] The "famished bolt" of lightning which flashes on this landmark does not signal the end of the march. It is, for the Leader, a favorable omen. The western provinces which lie beyond open a new future for mankind. In the morning, the heart of a black sheep is sacrificed, presumably to propitiate the powers which guide the march. In the following verses, the promises made in the opening Song are fulfilled. The paths of the world have been explored and the violent soul of man can at last experience the intoxication provided by the *Cocculus indicus*, possibly the bitter berries mentioned at the beginning of the poem.

XI *Canto IX. Man Returns to the Perishable Things*

The long desert journey led away from the "perishable things." They reappear in canto IX, in the form of the first smokes which signal human habitations and the presence of young women. One of them addresses the Leader. In the desert, man pursued eternal things. He now listens to the seductive call of temporal creatures. The woman who welcomes him announces alternately "the time of great heat" and "the time of a great blessing." Heat is associated with the end to the separation of man and woman and to sexual deprivation, with the ferment of pleasure generated in the bodies of women. The time of great blessing promised by the woman is expressed by a significant cluster of symbols: leaves, springs, vines, honey, a green star in a jar of cool water, night, and silence. If man, under the tent, is the "companion of the grave-corner," woman is associated with symbols of generation and rebirth which she places under the power of man. At the end of the long march, at the end of the day, is woman the promise or the illusion that life will prevail? The curious vision at the end of the canto could have the first meaning, since the canto which follows is a paean to the adventure of man, to life in all its manifestations: "—and erect on the shining edge of the day, on the threshold of a great land more chaste than death,/the girls made water straddling and holding aside their print gowns." The girls' gesture may seem indecent and vulgar, but it takes on a strange nobility. They are life itself, defiantly asserting itself against the nonhuman.

XII   Canto X. The Celebration of Man

The final canto is a recapitulation and a celebration. At the end of his *anabasis*, from the heights of the present, the Speaker turns back and surveys the achievements of centuries in the plains of the past. Three main divisions are mentioned. The first one deals with ritual acts or traditional customs having to do with death and generation, such as the sacrifice of colts on the graves of children or public acclamations for the exposure of bridal linen stained by defloration. A second category has to do with various kinds of activities necessary to maintain the life of the collectivity. They are summed up in the phrase "and the firesmoke of mankind everywhere . . . ," which expresses simultaneously the vanity of human enterprise and its conquering power. The third list is the longest. It is clearly an attempt to suggest the infinite variety of human experience. Men can be characterized in so many ways: by what they eat; by what they own; by the work they do; by what they sell; by what they make; by the games they play; by what they give away; by what they know; by what they have seen; by their art; by their vices; by their virtues; by their desires; by their pastimes. Any type of man may find himself listed here: toll collector or bee-keeper, gambler or lecher, craftsman or artist, scholar or hunter, hermit or soldier. The last-mentioned in this enumeration is the Storyteller who suddenly appears and settles all questions of precedence, possibly a figure of the poet. It would thus seem that poetry, for Saint-John Perse, is linked with the revelation of true values.

The Speaker has seen and evaluated all kinds of human achievements: collections of books and chronicles, the astronomer's workshop and the beauty of a graveyard, very ancient tem-

ples under palm trees. Beyond the reach of his vision, there have
been many secret actions. Some may have an impact on the future
of mankind: troop movements, ambushes, looting, and plotting.
Others have a less direct effect, although they may well be equally
significant: animals mating in the forest under the eyes of children, prophets convalescing in a stable, the silent conversations of
two men under the tree. With this final evocation, the poem re-
verts to its beginning, since its action was generated by such conversations. Beyond the actions of men, the Speaker also sees signs,
the seeds of the future, and the harvests to come until the female
star appears as a pure and sacred promise in the heights of the
sky. After the achievements of the past and the actions of man on
earth, beyond the portents of the future and the harvests of time,
man comes to the evening hour, to the nocturnal promise of the
dream: "Plough-land of dream! Who talks of building?—I have
seen the earth parcelled out in vast spaces and my thought is not
heedless of the navigator." The conquering spirit of man knows no
limit and will not be kept within the confines of a building, of a
city, of a civilization, of the universe itself. The world of dream
will always remain for him an open land, a fertile land.

XIII *Closing Song*

The structure, the situation, and the main themes of the closing
Song echo the opening Song. There are, however, a number of
significant changes. In the first stanza, the Speaker and his horse
have halted under a tree full of turtledoves. The birds are like
living leaves. In the morning, they are the glory of life itself. The
horse is no longer a colt: the life force which carries man forward
has reached its full power. The Speaker's whistling is so pure that
the rivers will keep faith with their banks. The rivers of time al-
luded to in cantos III and VI will not run dry. In the second
stanza, the Speaker recognizes that man may know sadness, but
sadness must yield to the splendor of the world. A man "arising
before day and biding circumspectly in the communion of an old
tree, leaning his chin on the last fading star, . . . beholds at the
end of the fasting sky great things and pure that unfold to delight. . . ." The ancient tree and the star, taken together, may
express the totality of Being, the earth and the sky, the past and
the future, reality and the dream. They are presented as necessary
supports which enable man to soar above the earth and to see

pure visions in the depths of the sky. As in the opening Song, the last stanza echoes the first one. The horse has stopped under the cooing tree, and the Speaker's whistling is still purer. To those who are about to die and who have not seen the perfection of this day, he wishes peace. The joy he has experienced may therefore reconcile man to his mortal fate. The concluding verses also tend to indicate that poetry is another form of conquest which enables man to bring a measure of sweetness into the lives of men.

XIV   *The Endless March to the Unknown*

In 1960, when Saint-John Perse was asked to define *Anabasis,* he reportedly gave this answer: "*Anabasis* has as its object the poem of loneliness in action. Action among men and action of the spirit, upon others as well as upon itself. I wanted to bring together the synthesis, not passive, but active, of human resourcefulness. But one does not treat psychological themes through abstract means. It was necessary to 'illustrate': it is the poem most filled with concreteness; this is why some have seen orientalism in it." In 1942, Saint-John Perse had already proclaimed his "fierce hatred of literary exoticism": "Of Asia, and especially of Central Asia, extraplanetary and extratemporal, I can say to you, like a pedant, that it gave me a broadened gauge of space and time." Twenty years later, he again stressed his contempt for the mere picturesque: "It has been said that I wandered through the desert out of interest for erudition or archeology. What attracted me there was only a mode of animal and natural life in touch with eternal things, as always the desert." [10] The Speaker of *Anabasis* is the figure of "human resourcefulness." He is the quintessential hero who, throughout the ages, has forced himself and others to live, to struggle and to die for the goal he has chosen. He is the mover of mankind. Without him, there would be only stagnation and death. Through him, history is made. Alain Bosquet describes him as a synthetic figure: he is simultaneously a military leader, like Alexander and Genghis Khan, a critical thinker and his own historian, like Xenophon, a man of action inspired by a grand design, a mystic and a visionary, like Isaiah and Moses.[11] The figure of the Speaker appears as a most appropriate symbol for the living energy which drives man to action, which compels him to go beyond his own limits, to explore all the possibilities open to man.

It is not impossible to see in *Anabasis* the poetic expression of theories frequently held by philosophers of history. According to Renan, for instance, history is the struggle of mankind toward a total knowledge of itself, toward the full realization of man's latent potential. Bergson's views on the dynamics of creative evolution, Toynbee's vision of history, or Teilhard de Chardin's dialectic of the human phenomenon (not to mention Hegel's and Marx's) could also be compared to Saint-John Perse's *anabasis* of man. The expedition described in *Anabasis* would then symbolize the progress of mankind toward higher forms of civilization, if not of life. It would also express the exploration and the conquest of man by that most exemplary of men, the poet. The military expedition is a fitting representation for the action of the soul upon itself. It is a symbol of spiritual struggle and conquest. In *Anabasis*, the epic of a hero thus becomes the epic of mankind striving forward and crossing the deserts of time in order to reach the distant shores of the future. It is significant that Saint-John Perse prefers to speak of the "human march," not of the human condition. Man is for him the "insatiable migrant." [12] *Anabasis* illustrates the archetypal conflict between stasis and movement, between temporality and eternity, between the concrete reality of the world and the spiritual urge to go beyond that reality. Man lives in a perpetual state of tension. He can never remain the prisoner of a single image. From the primitive migrations of nomadic horsemen to the most complex urban societies, he has never ceased to explore all the paths of the world, the endless horizons which even death cannot close.

CHAPTER 4

From Exile to the Kingdom

WHEN Aristide Briand, then minister of foreign affairs, appointed Alexis Leger director of his Cabinet in 1925, the poet Saint-John Perse ceased all literary activities. He did not renounce poetry: he only decided not to publish his writings until he retired from public life. Between 1925 and 1942, foreign translations of *Praises* and *Anabasis* were the only publications which appeared under the name of Saint-John Perse. He believed, certainly with good reason, that the demands made of a leading French literary figure were incompatible with his professional responsibilities. His decision had unfortunate consequences. In June, 1940, Hitler's armies occupied Paris. Leger's hostility to the Nazis made him a prime target of the Gestapo. His apartment was ransacked, his manuscripts confiscated and presumably destroyed. In the collected works of Saint-John Perse, *Exile*, written in the summer of 1941, comes immediately after *Anabasis*, published in 1924: no mention is made of the destroyed poems, and we are left with a feeling of wonder and sadness, although Saint-John Perse himself never expressed grief over this loss.

Alexis Leger arrived in America on July 14, 1940. In November, the collaborationist Vichy government deprived him of his French nationality. In December, his property was confiscated. The man who, for fifteen years, had been the executor of French foreign policy became an alien in a foreign land, a man without a country. From 1941 to 1946, Saint-John Perse served as a consultant in French Literature at the Library of Congress. To these five years, we owe the great poems of exile, from *Exile* to *Winds*. When Saint-John Perse arrived in Washington, poetry was the furthest thing from his mind. Archibald MacLeish ventured to mention the opportunity for writing which his new position could offer him. Saint-John Perse replied, "almost harshly," that for him there could be no question of poetry again.[1] A few months later, poetry returned triumphant.

I Exile

The first canto of *Exile* alludes to the circumstances which surrounded the birth of the poem. On the (then) lonely shore of Long Beach Island, facing east toward the ocean, a beach-house had been placed at the poet's disposal by American friends. Some of the details given in the poem would seem almost prosaic, were it not for their symbolic significance. The keys left with the keepers of the lighthouse will open for the poet the doors of his exile. The barren beach is the concrete representation of his new condition. The world which he has entered is hostile, cruel, deserted by the gods. This is a place of spiritual death, the "ossuary of the seasons." The poet has chosen this "place glaring and null," where the barren sands reflect the arid emptiness of his soul. Paradoxically, the desert beach suddenly turns into the site of an epiphany. Divine fire strikes as a conquering god: "The spasms of lightning are for the rapture of Princes in Taurida." Iphigenia was abducted to serve as the priestess of Diana in the distant land of Taurida. Similarly, the god of the thunderstorm has captured the "Princes," the poet-heroes whom he would press into his service.[2] On the sands of exile, a demonic power suddenly pounces upon its chosen victims. The French word *ravissement* may mean abduction, delight, or rape, and all three meanings are to some extent suggested in the poem. The seizure of man by the mantic power of poetry is almost an act of sexual aggression: its violence leads to a new birth.

The second canto develops the theme of creation in the midst of emptiness. The wanderer in foreign lands will not seize on the "painted altar horn," possibly an allusion to the poet's refusal to enter the service of the conquering god. His own glory is on the sands. He is not in error when he chooses the barest place for assembling in the wasteland of exile "a great poem born of nothing, a great poem made from nothing." The theme of emptiness is powerfully expressed in a series of images which tend to demonstrate the vanity of all human action. There is a feeling of deep personal despair in these verses: "I have built upon the abyss and the spindrift and the sand-smoke. I shall lie down in cistern and hollow vessel,/In all stale and empty places where the taste of greatness lies buried." The Princes of exile may have, at one time, held more power than Roman emperors or great priestly castes. They have learned these bitter truths: "Where the sands go to their song, there go the Princes of exile,/Where there were high taut sails, there goes the wreck more silken than a lute-maker's dream,/Where there were great war deeds, there lies now whitening the jawbone of an ass,/And the sea all around rolls her noise of skulls on the shores,/And all things in the world to her are in vain, so we heard one night at the world's edge/From the wind's militias in the sands of exile. . . ." The lesson of the wind echoes the message of the Preacher.

There is, however, another wisdom to be found in the foaming sea, in the fermenting of the spirit which crackles like salt and quicklime, in the wild fury of the soul. The message of the wind is a fraud. The barren sands are not empty of life. The Stranger's soul is not doomed to sterility. The poet compares himself to a rider, lariat in hand, watching in the desert for signs of good omen, for the appearance of divine life. In the desert of his soul, morning "moves her prophetic finger through sacred writings." The poem is the sudden manifestation, in the midst of nothingness, of a supernatural presence which establishes contact with man. On the lonely beach, a primeval experience is repeated. Man has always been an exile to whom the world must miraculously reveal itself anew, not as the Waste Land, but as the Kingdom. Man is the Stranger who must forever discover anew that the relics of the past are the premises of the future. The word in French is spelled *prémisses:* it refers to the first propositions of a syllogism from which a necessary conclusion must follow. There is another word, *prémices,* which means firstfruits. The similarity of sound seems to indicate that the creative powers of Being are as assured as the certainty of logic.

The third canto is a magnificent hymn to the Eternal Return, to the never-ending surge of Being which manifests itself in poetic creation. The theme is emphasized through the use of parallel verses, analogous syntactical constructions, rhythmic patterns, and echoing sounds. They underline the link created by the imagery between the military exploits of great conquerors, the migrations of entire nations, the proclamation of new empires, and the birth of great Books: all are manifestations of the same cosmic force which drives man forever onward. This hidden energy would sweep him up like drunkenness, like a trance, like a breath, like a wave, uttering "one long phrase without pause forever unintelligible." The wave which rises higher and higher before it breaks and the gull forever on its wing embody the divine power in pursuit of the poet's soul. This modulation of the theme is a familiar one, almost a cliché: the poet pursued by inspiration.

Romantic poets, such as Alfred de Musset in the celebrated *Nuit de Mai*, addressed their Muse in this fashion: "Is it you whose voice is calling/My poor Muse! is it you?/O flower mine! O my immortal One/In whose chaste and faithful soul/Love of me can still remain!" For Saint-John Perse, the Muse is a "monster," a "wandering force," a "Beggarwoman" dogging the steps of the Prodigal. After his initial flight, the poet turns around and faces her onslaught. Why does he resist? He knows her faithlessness. He knows only too well the emptiness which comes after the ecstatic communion with the creative "breath of origin." He had listened to the message of the wind, he had accepted his fate, but he suddenly finds himself roused from the nihilism of resignation by the epiphany taking place in the midst of exile. The victorious return of inspiration is expressed by the image of the triumphant wave, of a devouring creature which must overcome the poet's resistance: "So great an altitude can never annul the sheer fall from thy sill, O Apprehender of swords at dawn,/O Handler of eagles by their angles, Feeder of women shrill in their iron plumes!" There seems to be a progression which leads to the poet's defeat. At dawn, the poet seizes swords. He opposes his own violence to the violence which threatens to engulf him. He next appears as the Handler of eagles: if this is an allusion to Ganymede, the poet is in conflict with the divine power which would carry him away. Finally, if the iron plume may be traced back to Vigny's poem *L'Esprit pur*, the shrill women are the devouring Muses. In the concluding lines of the third canto, the impending conception of the poem generates both horror and exultation. For the poet, there is no escape. The relentless power which pursues him will not give him peace until he has renounced all allegiance to his own humanity, until he has totally surrendered to the monstrous force which will conquer him.

There is, in canto IV, a return to the theme of exile and nothingness, to the fragility of human action, to the desertion of man by the sacred. Mantic force is again pictured as a girl calling in the night to the man whom she has chosen, as a woman crossed in love who departed in the morning to visit other thresholds, as a goddess whose faithlessness was well known to ancient priests and sibyls, as a beggarwoman, as a paramour who must go before daybreak and whose passage must not be revealed, as a deity whose visitation leaves only the "smoking ashes of incest." The sexual union of a human and a deity is presented as a transgression of the most fundamental prohibition. It can lead only to destruction and ruin. The marks of naked feet on the doorsill, among sacred writings, fragments of beautiful stories drifting away in the sky, the song which came to the poet's unwilling lips, the words inscribed on the sand, the ciphers written on his tablets, the illicit signs on the faces of great stone mirrors exposed in caves—all have been erased, all are now gone and forgotten. The "poems of the night" must share the fate of the "spouse of a night." Once again, the vanity of all things becomes the dominant theme: "So goes all flesh to the hairshirt of salt, ashen fruit of our vigils, and the spouse of a night shown out before the dawn. . . ." The poems of the night may have been like "the pure nautilus of free waters, the pure mobile object of our dreams": they have become like "the fossil wing entrapped in great amber vespers." Nothing is left of the divine visitor's fiery embrace but the "debris of feather, fingernail, dyed hair, impure linen." Nothing is left of the poems "born one evening in the lightning's fork" but the "faintest trace," like "ash in women's milk." Once again, the concluding verses lead to a paradox. The fiery poems of the night may have turned to ashes, but the poet resolves to create from these useless remains a "pure language without purpose," a "great delible poem."

The fifth canto does indeed open with the poet's resolution to recover the lost splendor which is evoked in terms reminiscent of *Pictures for Crusoe* or *Praises:* "My hands more naked than at birth, and lips more free, ear to the coral reef that sounds the lament of another age,/Behold, I am restored to my native shore. . . ." On the shores of exile, the poet discovers that "there is no history but the soul's, no ease but the soul's." A man's history is not the succession of events which make up his life, but his spiritual transformation which may be compared to the passing of a single day from dawn till dusk. In the morning, the poet feels restored to his native estate, to the condition of the child for whom it is the simplest thing to be there, to exist side by side with the frailest things, dry stalks and grains of sand, the tiniest seed-pod or insect.

Morning ends: "On skeletons of dwarf birds the childhood of the day departs, in the dress of the Isles. . . ." With the end of childhood comes the awareness of exile. The eye stares at the red sheath of fate across the empty sands. As time passes, the poet's disillusion is expressed in a striking metaphor: "And now day thickens like milk." A day which curdles like milk has lost its purity, its freshness. The decline of the day conveys the feeling of a lost splendor. Man no longer lives in the heights with birds of prey, which previously appeared as symbols of the divine. Tedium and sadness drive him to the desert "kingdoms of Arsace." His search for salt is a symbolic search for the lost presence: "But what is it then, Oh! what is it that in everything is suddenly wanting? . . ." The poet is fully aware that in the history of mankind many a century has been deprived of the divine presence. Similarly, the declining sun seems to be burying its coins in the sand. A storm is brewing in the gathering shadows which may also suggest the impending judgment of fate. Submerged ruins, or submarine formations which recall ruins, confirm the fragility of human conquests. Nothing is left of the Spanish Empire ("O presidios under the green waters!") but ruined fortifications now covered by the sea. The great limestone leaves which have grown on the constructions of man take on an ironical meaning: they are like "lace on the mask of death." Canto V thus leads again to one inescapable conclusion: the inevitability of human defeat, of man's exile. Canto VI, on the other hand, is a ringing affirmation of man's spiritual victory.

The true "princes of exile" are those men who, even in times of troubles, remain living proof of *la ressource humaine*. The entire canto is the poet's hymn of praise to the sung and unsung men who, in one way or another, create a nobler image of man. Saint-John Perse establishes no conventional hierarchy. He places on the same rank the astronomer and the technician who cleans the telescope lenses, the man who paints seamarks and the oceanographer, the man who watches for forest fires and the meteorologist. There are other men whose social utility is less apparent. Nevertheless, they add a most important dimension to the image of man. Such are the men who, when hostile armies invade the city, go up to the organs or rescue a rare hybrid of Himalayan bramble-rose, or those who, at sea, are awakened by the dry smell of a small sand flower. They are dreamers, impractical men who lead their mounts to the spring and themselves fail to drink. There is, among them but not above them, the artist himself "who enters the arena of his creation, uplifted in his whole being and, for three days, no one may look upon his silence save his mother, no one may have access to his room save the oldest of the servants."

Having paid homage to his peers, the poet assesses his own position. He is a Stranger stranded on the shores of exile, and as he listens to the West, he can already hear the prediction of his fate: "Precarious guest on the outskirts of our cities, you shall not cross the threshold of Lloyd's where your word has no currency and your gold no standard . . . /'I shall live in my name,' was your answer to the questionnaire of the port-authority. And at the money-changer you have nothing to show but that which is suspect,/Like those great iron coinages laid bare by lightning." The buried coins which lightning brings to the surface recall the poems "born one evening in the lightning's fork" and the coins buried in the sand "at the rising of shadows wherein the thunder's pronouncements ripen" (cantos IV and V). They have no use in the practical world. And yet, in the concluding canto, the poet confirms his commitment to the divine power of the thunderstorm.

A conflict is suggested, in canto VII, between the message of the lightning and the human allegiances which must be sacrificed to its call: to the Mother, and to the Beloved. Exile has always been the destiny of man, but a woman in love cannot be reconciled to this fate: she loathes the Barbary bird singing its alien song under her roof. As she listens in the distance to the receding storm which drives her man farther and farther away, her cry rises out in revolt and asserts the human claim to happiness. For man, however, the sweetness of woman's love can be a source of weakness: her claim must be silenced, lest his soul fall prey to the dubious "eagle of happiness." Significantly, the image of the Beloved is described in terms reminiscent of the nocturnal Muse. In the third canto, the poet's soul fled across the sand before the nocturnal Spouse. He must now decide between the conflicting demands made by human love and by the winged presence of the Muse. His choice is made: the break with the past must be accepted, although not without a pang: "Nitre and natron are themes of exile." In the Bible, nitre and natron are agents of purification (*Jeremiah II, 22*).[3] Exile also purifies man by making him totally free from all previous attachments.

On the empty sands of exile, the human soul can best respond to the challenge of the sacred, like a snake "coiled beneath the lightning's whip." The poet is the messenger of an occult power which he must keep alive among men. Such is, I believe, the meaning of his final message: "Veiled be the faces of our wives; raised be the faces of our sons; and the order is: wash the stone of your sills . . . I shall whisper low the name of the springs in which tomorrow we shall plunge a pure wrath." Women must veil their faces as a sign of mourning or perhaps so as not to distract men from their purpose. Sons will hold their heads high and face the lightning's whip. Doorsills must be washed of all traces of the past in order to welcome a new revelation. The last lines are the most obscure, although they clearly refer to the creative energy of passion, to the powers of rebirth and renewal to which only the divine violence of poetic revelation can give access.

Exile recounts a spiritual struggle which might well be compared to Rimbaud's *Season in Hell*. Driven into exile by the fury of history, cut off from his past and faced with an uncertain future, Saint-John Perse did not yield to the temptation of nostalgia and despair. At the end of his struggle, he faced the future with renewed strength. The poem ends with this simple verse: "And the time is come, O Poet, to declare your name, your birth and your race. . . ." *Exile* is a poem of self-discovery. The "Prince of exile," the "Peregrine," the "Prodigal," the "Outlaw" recognizes and assumes his true identity and his mission among men. He is the Poet, the man whose exclusive goal must be the pursuit of the Sacred.

II *Poem to a Foreign Lady*

The *Poem to a Foreign Lady* was written in Washington, D.C., during the latter part of 1942. It is clearly related to *Exile*, by its theme as well as by the date of its composition. The epigraph, "Alien Registration Act," refers to the legislation, passed in 1940, which requires foreigners residing in the United States to register with the Department of Justice and to report annually to the attorney general. The poet and the Foreign Lady, both refugees from war-torn Europe, had to comply with the provisions of this act. This legal formality must have been a painful reminder of their condition: they were aliens, people without a country. It was an official confirmation that exile had become for them a permanent way of life.[4]

The *Poem to a Foreign Lady* was probably inspired by a visit which the poet paid to her in the summer of 1942. The first canto re-creates his reflections as he approaches her house. The Foreign Lady belongs to the Spanish nobility. She now lives on an anonymous street which holds for her neither past nor future. Her wooden house is like an ark moored in the depths of the abyss. Her lamps are kept burning, even at noon, as though to hatch ever-renewed sufferings. The burning lamps may also be seen as a sign of perpetual mourning. The sultriness, the stagnation, the heavy silence of that summer day seem to express the arrest of time, the loss of hope.

The cause of the Lady's sorrow is symbolically suggested in this verse: "The trams worn out with use which went off one evening at the turning of the street, which went off on rails to the Atlantis countries. . . ." In 1942, the city of Washington was in the process of converting its system of public transportation from streetcars to buses. The streetcars which went off one evening at the corner of the street never returned. As they passed familiar landmarks for the last time, they sang "the yesterdays," they sang "the otherwhere," they sang "evil at its birth," they sang "the wooded Summer of young Capitals infested with cicadas," they sang of times and places as lost as fabled Atlantis. The implied comparison explains why Washington is described throughout the poem as a submerged city. Only the streetcar tracks are left at the Lady's door, these two rails "which have not said their last." The tracks without streetcars are an ironical reminder that the "yesterdays," the "otherwhere," are now forever lost. The canto ends with a verse which is repeated as a refrain at the end of each canto: " 'Rue Gît-le-coeur . . . Rue Gît-le-coeur . . .' sings softly the Alien One under her lamps, and there are there the mistakes of her Foreign Lady's tongue." "Rue Gît-le-coeur" means "the street where the heart lies buried." The name refers to the ancient custom of burying the heart not with the corpse, but in a separate place. The Foreign Lady is probably unaware of this meaning. "Rue Gît-le-coeur" may mean for her the place where the heart lies. It is the symbol of a cherished past. Repeating this name becomes a magical incantation intended to regain the lost past, to overcome exile and separation. It is of course an error to confuse objective reality and the wish. It is another error to use an incantation which itself refers to death and separation.

The second canto is the Foreign Lady's plea for understanding. To her visitor, she explains her appearance: it is not caused by tears, but by "that affliction of the eyes which comes to us in the end from the excessive fixity of the sword-blade on all the embers of this world, (O Sabre of Strogoff at the height of our eyelashes!)." Just as Michel Strogoff's vision, in Jules Verne's novel, was nearly destroyed by a white-hot blade held over his eyes, the Foreign Lady's eyes suffer from prolonged exposure to the fiery violence of the times. She then addresses her request to the poet of exile, to him who sings "all the banishments of the world," to sing for her "an evening song to the measure of [her]—pain," "a song of grace for [her] lamps,/a song of grace for the vigil and for the dawn darker at the heart of the althaeas." He is for her the "man of France" who can make her hear again, "among the cries of the martins and all the Ursuline bells, rising through the gold chaff and the dead powder of [his] Kings/a laughter of washerwomen in the little cobbled streets" of a French provincial town (possibly Pau, birthplace of Henri IV, where Saint-John Perse spent part of his young years). She refuses to take notice of all the things which might lead her to accept exile: the song of the bright red cardinal on the roof of her house, the squirrel on the veranda, the paperboy, the milkman, the nuns collecting for charity, and the unusual sight of two eagles hovering over the city. All this means nothing to her, weighing less in her bare woman's hands than "a key from Europe stained with blood." The key is a dual symbol. It represents both her past life and the violent break with this life.[5] The last verse echoes the conclusion of the first canto: " 'Rue Gît-le-coeur . . . Rue Gît-le-coeur . . .' softly sing the bells in exile, and there are there the mistakes of their foreigners' tongue." The soft tolling of bells probably reminds the Lady of the "Ursuline bells" of her youth. On the other hand, the innocent starling, although it is a bird commonly found in Europe, is viewed with suspicion for its "un-catholic appearance." There is some irony in the use of this adjective, which means strange or suspect as well as heretical. The For-

eign Lady rejects anything which could distract her for a moment
from her absorption with the past, from the ephemeral illusion
that she is again where her heart lies.

The third canto is the poet's response to the Lady's request. It
begins with the invocation: "Gods close by, bleeding gods, faces
painted and shut!" These unidentified figures seem to represent
the divinities which preside over the Lady's destiny. Her closed
shutters and her lamps burning through the day bear eloquent
witness to her obstinate refusal of exile. Three years have elapsed
since she came to this house, and her large trunks still remain
unpacked. She continues to hope that her exile will soon end, but
the futility of such expectations is emphasized by the pitiless re-
currence of natural phenomena, by their indifference to human
sorrow, by the repeated destruction of her illusory hopes: "In
Summer green as an impasse, in Summer green with such beautiful green, what third dawn, drunk with belief, opens its locust
wings?" Soon the September rains will pour into the river a harvest of summer's dead cicadas, the pitiful remnants of dead illusions. The expected dawn never came, the anticipated flight never
took place. Any attempt to stem the flow of time or to ignore its
devouring abyss is doomed to failure.

For Saint-John Perse, the Foreign Lady is Europe herself,
bleeding at the flanks like the Virgin of the Toril, pierced by seven
swords like Our Lady of Sorrows. She is the symbol of a dying
faith, a dying world which survives only in the petrified realm of
art, in the equestrian statues of knights to be seen in ancient
churches or in the paintings of Velásquez depicting forgotten vic-
tories. The poet honors her suffering. He also sees the degeneration of the aristocratic ideal and the secret flaw which led to its
corruption. Ultimately, were not the images of a glorious past as
deceptive as "that sign of happiness, on your gulfs too blue,/like
the gold palm-tree inside the boxes of cigars?" The poet will join
the Lady in mourning for the past, singing the lost yesterdays, the
"otherwhere," the "evil at its birth/and the splendour of living
that, this year, goes into exile out of reach of men." But on that
summer evening, he will not succumb to the stupefying atmosphere of death and exile which surrounds him, in this high dis-
trict where his route takes him past foundations for the blind,
enshrouded reservoirs and encaged cemeteries. He will grant the
Lady's request, he will sing a "song of grace" for her lamps. The

poet takes on the stature of a hero who challenges death and time as he sets out to "deliver the people of [her] lamps." The fireflies around his bare forehead like a crown of laurels are a sign of his victorious powers. He whistles to them as though he were Aeneas calling to a host of Sibyls, evoking the incredulous ghosts of his past. Like Aeneas carrying the Golden Bough, he has defied the abyss: "once more in dreams I pat with my hand, among so many invisible beings,/my hound-bitch in Europe who was white and, more than I, a poet." The poem concludes with this version of the refrain: "'Rue Gît-le-coeur . . . Rue Gît-le-coeur . . .' softly sings the Angel to Tobias, and there are there the mistakes of his Foreigner's tongue." Here again, the voice of the Angel takes the exile back to the place where his heart lies, but this miracle is only the magic of dreams. In the land of exile, the foreign words can only conjure up an illusory shadow.

In the Foreign Lady, the poet may have recognized a part of himself which he must exorcise, although its suffering deserves respect and even tenderness. Like Tobias, who delivered Sarah from the demon Asmodeus, he will accomplish his self-appointed task: in the depths of the abyss, he will delived the Foreign Lady's lamps from their burden of sorrow and re-create for her the lost homeland. As for him, like Aeneas after his descent to the underworld, he is resolved to accept exile as his homeland. The fascination with the past leads to morbid self-absorption and to the rejection of life itself. The poet is lucid enough not only to recognize the inevitability of historical becoming but also to perceive the limitations of former ideals. He can still surround himself with the invisible ghosts of bygone days, but he walks with a "free man's stride, without horde or tribe, amidst the song of the hourglasses." His fidelity to the past has not become a prison. Unlike the Lady, he has resumed the human march, accompanied by the music of time.

III *Rains*

The theme introduced in the concluding verse of *Exile*, purification and regeneration, becomes the central theme of *Rains*. The poem was written in 1943, as Saint-John Perse was traveling in Georgia with American friends. A tropical storm provided a new encounter with the demonic forces of inspiration. The sudden appearance of the torrential rains is expressed in the first canto by the image of a giant tree growing over the entire city: "The banyan of the rain takes hold of the City. . . ." The rains thus become a living entity, a monstrous creature which establishes its dominion over the world of men. On the ground, the splashing rain is a "milk of living water" where a "hasty polyp rise to its coral wedding," suggesting the emergence of powerful sexual and generative energies. The same forces are at work within the poet. They create a vision where sensuality and animality combine with the violence of a Roman circus scene. As in *Exile,* the conception of a poem is experienced almost as an act of sexual aggression which is both welcomed and feared. The imagery creates an atmosphere of unbridled sexual license and fertility, mixed with the themes of purification and regeneration.

In *Rains,* Saint-John Perse rediscovers the archetypal association of water with the primordial substance from which all forms were born. If the splashing rain is a "hatching of golden ovules in the tawny night of the slime," the poem is an "obscene rose" which "livens and grows and curls." On the edge of such dreams, the poet's bed is made, "O fraud!" Poetic revelation is thus compared to the mystery of sexuality, to a perilous and forbidden discovery illicitly procured. The poet then calls on the "terrible Lord" of his laughter. This enigmatic entity is not clearly identified: it may embody the Dionysiac forces unleashed by the rains, the poet's wild exultation in his transgression. The virgin water washes the earth clean of human steps. The smell of clay, like the smell of wine, brings on the loss of memory. The past is erased. The rains are the magic substance which restores the "used up earth" to its primeval fertility. A similar process takes place within the poet's soul. This is, I believe, what is expressed in the concluding verses, which bring together the "Earth used-up, the new hour in its swaddling-clothes," and the poet's heart "host to a strange vowel."

In canto II, the poet questions the Rains. They are, for the man whom they have elected, "most suspect Nurses, Waiting-women with veiled elder eyes" whose attention makes him "unusual," a member of a separate caste. He becomes the *voleur de feu* who asks the Rains "on what new bed, from what stubborn head" men can steal the "valid spark." Receiving no answer, the poet still chooses to cast his lot with the Rains. The points of their spears will decide his fortune. Poetic creation is again expressed through images introduced in the first canto: foam at the lips of the poem like coral milk, and the Idea, "dancing like a snake-charmer," "naked as a sword-blade" at the chariot races. The nascent poem appears as a Pythoness foaming at the mouth (there is a reference, in canto I, to the "Prophetic Virgins"), but the Idea will teach the poet "ceremony and measure against the poem's impatience." Piercing and cutting weapons are the instruments of a spiritual battle. The outcome of the struggle will decide whether the wild energies of elemental forces can be tamed.[6]

Once again, the poet calls on the "terrible Lord" of his laughter, not, however, to exult in the demonic unleashing of primitive energies, but to be spared "the avowal, the welcome and the song." The onslaught of cosmic waters dissolves the illusions, the deceptions, or the lies which are part of man's loftiest endeavors. The rains put out the fire in the hearth, the lamps in his hands. Nothing is left of man's boldest speculations on "the essence of being." In the confrontation with the elemental forces at work in nature and within man, the pretensions of reason are reduced to curls of smoke, and human claims to knowledge soon revert to darkness.

In canto III, the Rains assume other identities. They are female conquerors marching across the earth, carrying spears like ancient Assyrian warriors. They are queens magnificently arrayed, deserted by their faithless lovers, like Dido trampling ivory at the gates of Carthage or Cortez' Indian wife, Malinche, "heady with clay and painted, among her tall apocryphal plants." They are warriors and dancers. The violence of war, revolution, and sex with which they are associated is brought forth in a powerful series of images: weapons by the armloads, girls by cartloads, a presentation of eagles to the Roman legions, a rising of pikes during the French Revolution of 1789, unbound sheaves of dissolute virgins, a bountiful harvest in the arms of men. The themes of renewal, fertility, and sex recur in the final verses, where the Rains also bring knowledge and create beauty.

The gift of the Rains, in canto IV, is a new language. They bring to man the almost unbearable ecstasy of a speech which is "like the very breath of the spirit, like the thing itself proffered,/Flush with being, its essence, flush with the spring, its birth." The French word *proférer* means to utter, but Saint-John Perse was undoubtedly aware of the etymological meaning of the

Latin *proferre,* which has been preserved in English. The message
of the Rains is an epiphany ("Ah! the full shower of the health-
giving god on our faces. . . ."). Here again, the experience of the
holy remains associated with the notion of transgression. The
Rains are "most suspect Nurses," "Simoniacs" trafficking in holy
things. They have descended among men to bring them what men
had been denied, the fatal dream of another condition, the revelation of divinity. In the celestial heights, the Rains have consorted
with "lust-leap lightning." On the pure vellum of the sky lined by
its divine sparking, they have seen its "great uncial of green fire."
They appear as courtesans ready to betray to mere men the holy
secrets of the gods. A symbolic relationship is suggested between
the sacrilegious rains, birds caught in a hailstorm and stoned to
death on the cross of their wings, and fallen angels struck by divine vengeance.

In canto V, the approach of the Rains no longer seems to arouse
the same enthusiasm. The "men of the cities" had dreamed of
"more lofty confidences at the first breath of the rainstorm." Their
expectation was not fulfilled. The Rains only made them aware of
their human limits: "you give us back, O Rains! to our human
urgency, with the clay taste under our masks." The question then
is asked: "In higher places [*en de plus hauts parages*] shall we
seek memory? . . . or must we sing oblivion to the gold bibles of
the lower foliage?" The verse is highly ambiguous. *Hauts parages*
may mean high lineage as well as high places. The "gold bibles of
the lower foliage" contrast with the "great uncial of green fire"
written by lightning on the vellum of the sky. They can also be
opposed to the "thin slag heaps" of the cities, to the meager debris
of human civilizations. The poet may be asking: will man be
faithful to the divine revelation of the lightning, to the memory of
a higher condition, or will he pledge his allegiance to the gospel of
the earth? He may also be saying: should not man forget the dead
remains of history and listen to the revelation of the living foliage,
of the elemental clay from which he came? There is, I believe,
some irony in this ambiguity.

The irony is pursued in the following verses, with their images
of sickness, stagnation, decay, and impotence. Such are the themes
of those who have chosen to remain within the protective confines of the past. They have stayed in the orchard of their childhood, on the ancient tree where the lovely widows of lightning,

the Rains, are not allowed to bring their disturbing message. These men live in the "insipid season of the unerrant man," on the "earth tired of the mind's burns," weary of the searing brand of the spirit. The "green rains" are bringers of life. They wash away the woman-ish idols of the past and inspire the foundation of new empires. Men must free themselves from the weight of centuries. They must forget prestigious dynasties, the dead of former wars, the dreams of revenge, the old glories and the old lies. The poet betrays his impatience with the claims of the past, with the "smoke of charred history's exploits" which still lingers among the smoldering embers of the age. For Baudelaire and Mallarmé, for Gottfried Benn and T. S. Eliot, the hospital and the sickroom were fitting metaphors of the modern world.[7] Saint-John Perse recognizes the sickness and the impotence of a dying culture, but in its "Charterhouses and Leperhouses," "bedridden Princes" rise from their wattles: "Once, once I had a taste for living among men, but now earth breathes out its alien soul. . . ." For the risen Princes, there is a higher loyalty than the claims of a decaying civilization. And yet, can man renounce all human allegiances? This conflict is the dominant theme in canto VI.

A man who has smelled the "alien soul" of earth under the rains no longer cares for glory or power among men. He will indeed raise "sponge and gall to the wounds of an old tree laden with the chains of the earth," he will hasten the passing of the old order. As in *Winds,* the dying tree appears as a symbol of cosmic death. At this point, however, this echo is heard: "Once, once I had a taste for living far from men, but now the Rains . . ." What, then, is the lesson of the Rains? They appear, in the remainder of this canto, as figures of mystery: "Fugitives with no message," "face-less Mimes," "Half-breeds" divided between heaven and earth. They remind man of his own divided nature. They mirror his fas-cination with elemental forces: the dark enigma of sex, the over-powering energy of vegetation which suddenly invades the city of lifeless stone, the forgotten sweetness of the wilderness. This does not mean that the poet (who speaks for man) surrenders to the gods of the rainstorm. He may "drink of divinity," but his "lip is made of clay." Such is the true mission of the Rains: they wash away the superfluous legacy of the past, its misleading lessons and its false gods. Once again, the earth emerges as an unadulterated text which can at last be read in its authentic form. The Rains pass by and men return to their age-old ways, but they pay homage to their mysterious Visitors. Canto VII is their hymn of praise.

The Rains are called on to cleanse the eyes, the hearts, and the hands of men, to free them from the shackles of the past, to make them strong again. The Rains must wash away the obstacles in the "path of action," the obstruction in the "field of vision": the film from the eyes of the righteous man, of the man of good taste, of the man of talent, of all the men so inhibited by doubt and caution, by conventional prudence and decency, that they dare not act, that they cannot see. The Rains must wash away the "benevolence from the hearts of the great Intercessors, the seemliness from the forehead of the great Educators," the hypocrisy and the lies which allow the "great Intercessors," the "great Educators" to become accomplices of oppression and exploitation. The Rains must wash away the paralyzing weight of past history, annals and chronicles, bulls and charters, yellowing vellums and parchments. Finally, the Rains must wash away the fossilized remnants of a dead culture for which men still retain a perverted taste: "roundelays and elegies," "villanelles and rondeaux," "Attic salt and euphuist honey," the literary debris which clutter the "hearts of men most gifted for the great works of reason."

In canto VIII, the "wandering thing on the winds of heaven" which came down to live among men has gone. Lightning did not strike. The expected revelation was not made. And yet, the visitation of the Rains was not in vain. As in the preceding cantos, their passage is associated with sexuality and fertility, with life-giving violence, with the intrusion of the sacred, with the animal splendor of desire. The Rains also appear as the sudden influx of inspiration, as the creating, foaming waters which overcome the poet and are gone before the poem is born.

In the concluding canto, a question is asked which echoes the alternative presented in canto V: "Night come, the gates closed, what does sky-water weigh in the lower empire of the copsewood?" A doubt is raised: can the heavenly Rains have any significance in a decadent world, in a fragmented world, in a world plunged in darkness? The poet gives his answer: as in canto II, the "points of the lances" will decide his fortune. If all things are equal on the "scales of the mind," if logic or reason cannot settle the matter, the poet will choose conflict. For the last time, he calls on the "terrible Lord" of his laughter to take up the quarrel to a higher place, to wage his battle "at the arid threshold of the poem," where his laughter scares "the green peacocks of fame." Here again, the meaning remains elusive. It is clear, however, that poetic revelation has nothing to do with the pursuit of worldly fame. It is associated with division and conflict, with scandal and violence. The birth of a poem is the work of primeval forces which can only be compared with the untamed energy of nature, war and sex, with the awesome visitation of the sacred.

IV *Snows*

Snows is the last poem in the bilingual edition of *Exile*. It bears the indication "New York City, 1944." Saint-John Perse dedicated the poem to his mother, from whom he had been separated for nearly four years. *Snows* shares several characteristics with the *Poem to a Foreign Lady*. Both works evoke a large American metropolis. Both are associated with one season of the year. Both are dedicated to a woman who appears as a figure of the past. Both have the deliverance from the past as a central theme.

The first canto of *Snows* is a striking re-creation of a winter dawn over New York City. Snow has been falling through the night. Under the feathery accumulation, the tall buildings have grown taller and lighter, as though the entire city had been freed from the burden of its weight. Skyscrapers with their lighted windows give the impression of pumice stone bored through by luminous insects. The silent dawn is compared to "a great fabulous owl under the breath of the spirit, swelled out in its white dahlia body." Snow, like lightning, rain, wind and storms, appears as a manifestation of sacred forces in nature, as an epiphany. The first coming of the snow is also likened to "that mist of breath at its birth like the first shiver of a sword bared." The poet's imagination re-creates a typical cluster of images which combines symbols of verticality, flight, whiteness, cutting weapons and spiritual revelation.[8] A religious tone is maintained throughout the canto through the use of expressions with characteristic connotations: "all their affliction remitted unto men of memory," "a place of grace and of mercy," "the souls' burden," "marvel and festival," "let there be salutation on the face of terraces." In French, the religious tone is still more pronounced, since *avoir charge d'âmes* means to have the cure of souls as well as the souls' burden, and *salut* means salvation as well as salutation. *La sixième heure* is the biblical way

of expressing time. Like the Saviour, the snow has come to deliver
men from their affliction. Its action is also similar to the power of
poetic visitation: it enables man to forget, at least for a moment,
the misery of mankind. Its coming provides the poet with a "for-
tuitous haven," a "place of grace and of mercy for releasing the
swarms of the great odes of silence." Poetic creation is thus related
to the swarming of bees. This symbol plays a significant role in the
works of Saint-John Perse, where it often occurs in relation with
the generative power of life and the propagation of cosmic
energy.

In the second canto, the poet appears divided between his
awareness of human suffering and the ecstasy brought by the pure
splendor of the snows: "I know that ships in distress in this wide,
pale oyster-spat thrust their lowing of deaf beasts against the
blindness of men and gods; and the whole world's wretchedness
calls the pilot off the estuaries." This verse may well allude to the
bleakest days of World War II, when the world was indeed calling to America for help. The snow, on the other hand, is described
through images which express the sacred beauty of a world indifferent to the vicissitudes of history. At the waterfalls of great
rivers (such as Niagara), "strange alliances" take place between
sky and water, "white nuptials of noctuids, white festivals of may-
flies." In the Great Lakes region, where defense plants were kept
in continuous operation, the lights burning through the night appear as marvelous fruit growing on a "sidereal trellis across the
espalier of the sky." The snow-covered lamps are "raw silk things
of snow," gigantic white cocoons. In another image, the snow becomes a "wide, pale oyster-spat," while in deeper waters wide
fields of mother-of-pearl seem to prepare their reply, the rebirth
of all things, the "vision at last without fault or flaw."

The sacred essence of the snows is indicated in another verse:
"on the vast railway-stations smoky with dawn like palm-groves
under glass, the milky night begets a mistletoe-feast." The mistle-
toe, the use of which has been preserved in connection with
Christmas festivities, is reminiscent of the celebrated Golden
Bough which was believed to be the repository of divine Life. The
falling snow restores the primeval purity of Being. Whatever hap-
pened since the origins of time is erased. It snows on the new idols
of men, on the product of their feverish industry, on the "gods of
alloy" and the "steelworks lashed with brief liturgies." The snows

extend their dominion over the entire continent, over the creations of nature and the works of men, over cruelty and gentleness, over goodness and evil, over past and future, over space and time. The realm of the snows lies "outside Christendom." They re-create a world where the presence of the sacred is felt without any mediator. Through them, the world appears in its original splendor to the poet's soul, as the divine bridegroom to his bride: "Spouse of the world, my presence." In the ecstasy of this revelation, human sorrow may be resented as an unwelcome intruder: "And somewhere in the world where silence illuminates a larch-tree's dream, sadness raises its servant mask."

It must be noted, however, that a parallel verse occurs in the third canto, which refers to the poet's mother: "And She whom I think of among all the women of my race, from the depths of her old age raises to her God her face of gentleness." The pure vision created by the snows nearly caused the poet to forget the humble suffering of women. Instead of the primeval perfection of Being, the limitless expanse of the snows comes to represent the vastness of space and time which separates the poet from his past, the prolonged absence so cruel to the "hearts of women where hope wastes away." Exile from the ancestral past is expressed in terms borrowed from medieval law: "For our years are lands in tenure which no one holds in fief. . . ." All through the long years of separation, his mother alone had the power to overcome the "black stone" of silence in his heart, to make him hear again the "pure song" of his lineage. The poet thus appears divided between the fascination of the snows and the "agony of sweetness" which the memory of his human heritage reawakens in his soul, between the "plain chant of the snows" and the "song of pure lineage."

Paradoxically, this opposition is emphasized by a number of parallel features which express similarity rather than contrast. The pale flowers of brambles which remind the poet of his mother's eyes also recall the whiteness of the snow. The religious vocabulary and the symbolic connotations associated with the snows are echoed in the hymn to the Mother. Such similarities, however, only serve to emphasize a deeper opposition. The "Lady of high lineage" is now a "poor woman in her old age," a martyr in her captive land, without a man to protect her, without a church to comfort her: "In the heart of the beautiful land where we shall burn the thorn, it is indeed a great pity for the women of every age whose men's arms have failed them. And who is it will lead you, in this great widowhood, to your Churches underground, where the lamp is frugal and the bee divine?" Saint-John Perse makes it quite clear that he does not share his mother's faith. The God to whom she prays is her God, not his, but he understands the deep meaning of her religion: the frugal lamp and the divine bee suggest the victory of light over darkness, the triumph of life over death, of spirit over matter. His own beliefs are expressed in a parallel series of symbols: "A lamp/survives the cancer of the night. And a bird of pink ash, which was a burning ember all summer, suddenly lights up the crypts of winter, like the Phasis Bird in the Hour Books of the Year One Thousand. . . ." In the dark night of history, life itself appears as a sign of illuminating grace, as a promise that the world will not end.[9] If the revelation of the snows is but an illusion, the poet will embrace it: "Spouse of the world, my presence, spouse of the world, my vigil! May the fresh wind of falsehood ravish us once more! . . ."

The last canto is the triumphant celebration of the Promised Land. Alone in his corner room where he has found a temporary shelter, the poet compares himself to explorers ready to set out in their frail canoes on the ocean of the snows. Each day takes them farther from the place of their birth, as they progress farther and farther inland, following the rivers toward their sources. Each day, they know better the "course of illegible things," until they are "caught up suddenly into that harsh glare in which all language loses its power." Saint-John Perse thus creates a significant link between the journey of life, the deciphering of illegible signs, the pursuit of origins, and the revelation which comes when man reaches the source of language itself. His undertaking is described as a break in the cosmic order, as a perilous quest for the "primal waters" toward which he wanders, "like the traveller at the new moon whose direction is uncertain and his gait aberrant."

The primitive language which the poet is pursuing as he ascends along that "pure unwritten delight where runs the ancient human phrase" is not any hypothetical *Ursprache*. He is no philologist bent on reconstructing the primitive parent language from which all others are derived. He is a poet searching for the ultimate source of speech, for the *arché* which by definition escapes all definition. It can only be suggested in a series of symbols: "a beautiful country without hatred or meanness, a place of grace and of mercy," "a great *Ave* of grace," "the great white-rose gardens of all the snows," "freshness of umbels, of corymbs, freshness of aril under the bean," "so many wafers still." The *archê* to which he aspires is the "new flora" which delivers us from "the flower and from the fruit," from the burden of temporal becoming. It is the "dwarf-elder of dream," the reward given at long last to the "spouse of the world, our patience," "the fresh wind of falsehood" which comes to our souls from the "great linens of dreams and all that fungible wealth in which man involves his fortune." The "linens of dream," fresher than any linen woven by "bone shuttle in the hands of very old women" or by "ivory almond in the hands of very young women," stand in opposition to the shroud of death or the web of love. They merge into the "page on which no more is written." *Snows* thus appears as a symbolic return to the mythic origin of time, as the poet attempts to make of the present a new beginning. The "snows of absence" open for man the dimension of dream, the limitless space where the "great human phrase" still remains unwritten. The empty surface of the snow is, very simply, the space of poetry, the paradoxical space where the "snows of absence" lead to the total presence, and the purification of nothingness to the fullness of Being.

IV *The Meaning of Exile*

With the fall of France in 1940, a world had suddenly come to an end. In the space of a few months, Saint-John Perse had been deprived of his position, his possessions, his country, his poems, his loved ones. The break with the past was complete. The four poems of *Exile* are linked by a common theme. They celebrate the ordeal of exile as a purifying ritual which reopens for man the ways of the divine. In the epiphany of poetic revelation, the alien land miraculously becomes the Kingdom where the Sacred reveals its presence.

CHAPTER 5

The Epic of Mankind

IN 1919, at the end of World War I, Valéry voiced his doubts about the future of European civilization. At the close of World War II, Saint-John Perse questioned the future of man himself. The use of the atom bomb, in 1945, had demonstrated that man held in his hands the means of destroying not only civilization, but life itself. *Winds,* which bears the date 1945, thus appears as an epic meditation on the fate of man: is he doomed to extinction, or does he still have a future? *Winds* is the passionate proclamation of the poet's faith in the Eternal Return of life renewing itself through the worst upheavals of history.

I   *Book I. The Cycle of Death and Rebirth*

The winds evoked in the first canto have an essential purpose: the joyful and violent expulsion of the old so that the new may come into being. An age is reaching its end, represented in the poem by a "whole century . . . rustling in the dry sound of its straw." Just as the life force has gone from the dried up straw, divinity has deserted "the heart of men in office" and "the great works of the spirit." The winds blow relentlessly over the whole world, scenting out death wherever it may lie undetected, in a royal palace or a monk's cell, amid wealth or poverty, on the squares of the cities or at the blind archways of the Offices, thus revealing its presence at the very heart of civilization. Since the word "Offices" may refer to public office, to religious ceremonies, or to the celebrated Uffizi museum, its use suggests that public institutions, religion, and art are no longer alive.

Through successive metaphors, a dying age is compared to a great tree in its "rags and remnants of last winter," to a beggar who has squandered its inheritance, to a "magical tree" proudly wearing its "icons and fetishes," the "shells and spectres of locusts," to the "tree of language" fallen into its dotage. The im-

88

agery implies little respect for the legacy of the past. A doomed civilization is *à bout de cosses, de siliques:* having run out of seeds, it is fated to sterility. Its past glories are faded. Its noblest creations have become empty shells deserted by the "wings and swarmings" which the "wind of heaven" carries away. For the sacred spirit of life, the tree and its dead harvest are but *lais et relais,* a barren space cluttered by debris abandoned by the receding wave, a temporary resting place forsaken for a new departure. The language of a dying age may still be proud of its "oracles and maxims," but in the "quincunxes of knowledge," its speech is the "murmur of one born blind."

The tree also stands for the Cosmic Tree. Its death is the death of the world. The symbol, however, implies that this death is not final. A new world, a new age will take its place. Finally, the tree is the human soul, seared by love and violence, its energy spent, but ready to sing once again the song of desire as the wind blows through "its rattles of dead wood and its corollas of baked clay." Like the tree, the paper on which the poem is written rustles in the wind of poetic creation. The birth of poetry is thus presented as another manifestation of the sacred energy symbolized by the winds. According to primitive beliefs, these forces had to be propitiated through ritual invocations and sacrifices. The creation of the poem is described as the performance of such a ritual.[1]

At the end of the first canto, an invocation is addressed to the powers which will inspire the poet. In canto II, the poet assumes the persona of the Narrator. His sacred office is emphasized by his identification with a Shaman dressed for the ritual sacrifice. The Shaman has eaten the "rice of the dead," but his "word is for the living": he embodies the victorious challenge of life to death. To his audience, the Narrator makes a similar promise: the regeneration brought by the storm. Through the imagery, the mantic powers of poetry are also linked with primitive rites of divination, with the sudden irruption of Dionysiac forces, with possession by a god.

The winds, in the third canto, are revealed as the sacred manifestation of the instinctive energies of life. As they run riot throughout the world, they fulfill a ritual function: they break up the old forms; they restore the fertility of the primeval Chaos; they shape a new future free from the deadening restraints of the past. In the age-old conflict of nature and culture, Saint-John

Perse sides with the forces of instinct. He takes an iconoclastic delight in the action of the winds as they strike down the most respected institutions of the past, be they religious (baptistery or pagoda), political (the Roman Senate or the Kingdom of France), or cultural (the *ruelles* strewn with engravings, incunabula, and letters from women).[2] The winds may bring destruction, but they liberate the creative energies imprisoned by the old forms. Their violent presence is felt everywhere, from revolutionary uprisings to the unrestrained amusements of city crowds. Other associations link the life force of the winds to the exploration of a New World, to the unused energy latent in wild life, in our neglected animality. The winds are that restlessness which will not allow life to remain stagnant, the dreams which lure it toward the unknown, away from familiar landmarks.

In primitive religions, rituals of regeneration often took the form of a collective orgy. Accepted norms, limits, distinctions, or prohibitions were rejected. All barriers were broken so that the life energy could circulate freely. For Saint-John Perse, the winds serve a similar purpose. He cannot show enough contempt for the "casemates on the frontiers, low as pigsties, and the custom-houses down lower still to the sloping of the earth." By removing all artificial boundaries, divisions, and classifications, the winds restore the integrity and fertility of origins, aptly suggested by a "hundred virgins and aurochs." The *stèles votives* are also *stèles fautives*. What guilt do they betray? They show that civilizations presumed to impose a false design on the true face of the earth. The winds unravel the "living works from the dead." They uncover the "new scriptures enclosed in the great schists of the future." Through a complex network of metaphors, the future of mankind is linked to the revelation of new sacred texts, to the awakening of priestesses, to the moulting of winged girls, to the metamorphosis of nymphs, and—through a play on the dual meaning of the word "nymph"—to the epiphany of the bee coming out of the chrysalis. This vision of metamorphosis seems to suggest the possibility, for man, of rising to a higher estate. Such is the inebriating power of the dream: it frees man from the limits of his humanity.

The poet's mission is defined in the opening verse of canto IV: "All to be done again. All to be told again. And the scything glance to be swept across all man's heritage." Total destruction is the prerequisite of total regeneration. The man who laughs at the

"Librarians' stone galleries" is ridiculing the dead gods from which man must be liberated. The Librarians are like the priests of Serapis who served in the great Library of Alexandria, but their gods are only dead gods stuffed with straw. No living deity inhabits their Basilica of marble and bronze, their sterile world of stone and metal. The dust of archives is like the dust accumulated over the ruins of holy cities. The powder which settles over the books neatly lined on their shelves is equated to "all things scaling off toward nothingness, deposits of the depths over their faeces, slime and dregs at the very bottom of silt—ashes and scales of the spirit." If man is to live, he must escape.

In the fifth canto, the ritual exorcism of the past is accomplished. The canto opens with an invocation to Eâ, the Babylonian god of the watery Chaos to which all things must revert. The poet sees himself in that interval between the end of an age and the dawn of another, when civilizations fade away like elegant ladies at the end of a ball. He shows no regret for a vanishing past, only a slight contempt which is quite apparent in the imagery. He is no Musset doing a farewell gala for a dead opera singer. His stanza is "light on the traffic of years," like the "chant of the vendor of gaufres in the wake of advancing armies, at the upsetting of the tables of Merveilleuses, of Dandies," a fitting image for the refined artificiality of a superannuated way of life doomed by the march of historical necessity. The birth of a new age is expressed by the "new fonts," which suggest a newborn child as well as the spiritual birth of baptism or the emergence of new waters. The dead past must be destroyed: books are thrown into the rivers, lamps into the street, and the poet-shaman, on the rooftop, watches for the regenerating storm.

A central element in the rituals of regeneration is the *hieros gamos*, the sacred union of a mortal and a god. The highest knowledge does not come from books on their racks, "sad as servants and hired girls." In their place, there will be a "bed of iron for a naked woman, all the bays open to the night," "a woman very beautiful and chaste" for the embrace of the god. The poet-shaman waits, like the woman, for the revelation which will come to him from the sky. The end of canto V develops this identification of poetic creation and divine visitation. The poet now appears as the Enchanter who "takes counsel with the new conspiracies in the bed of the wind." Like the woman on her bed of iron, he awaits the coming of the god. The Eastern sky in the morning seems to offer the promise of rebirth, and the "Western sky takes on the image of the great floods." The message of the wind is a "counsel of force and violence." The forces at work in the upheavals of history or in poetic revelation have the same divine origin. They are destructive forces, but also, like the winds and the floods, agents of purification and rebirth.

The conclusion of canto III is echoed at the beginning of canto VI: "Drunken, the more drunken, you were saying, for denying drunkenness. . . ." Of the three men who speak in this canto, each welcomes the Dionysiac powers of the winds, each welcomes the destruction they wreak. The first one to speak brings a message for the "living," for new men who have no use for the "repudiated hour," for men from the "lower districts" whose turn has come to claim their due. New leaders must be found, men from the "Marches," "men of great power reduced by inaction to the profession of Enchanter." The French word for Marches is *confins*, which may indicate either that the ancient order had excluded these men from its midst, or that these men had advanced to the extreme limit of human experience, or both. Saint-John Perse may be thinking of charismatic prophets and leaders as well as of poets when he describes them as "men assailed by the god," "men nourished on new wine and as though transfixed by lightning." The first speaker is the voice of action, and action is born of impatience and violence, of intolerance and secession. The gods of the winds are warlike gods: the action they inspire is likened to the edge of swords, to the point of arrows. The dead and the bankrupt are those who fail to face the wind, to move forward to the frontiers of the human, to reach for the divine fire. Life is thus depicted as the struggle of man to go beyond the narrow limits of his condition. He who fails to do so betrays his mission.

The second speaker is the "Babouvist philosopher," the revolutionary leader who comes to the fore when "all things are torn loose," when all men raise their heads to the rising of new signs. The city, with its collieries and its harbor installations, is an obvious symbol of the modern industrial age. For Saint-John Perse, this age is doomed. The forces which will destroy it are represented by the lightning which strikes three times, like the flashing of a sword. This destruction is implicitly justified, since the city is a "golgotha of scrap iron and garbage" on which man is crucified. The "Babouvist philosopher" calls for the rebirth of men dehumanized by the vile era which ends beneath the lightning flash. Men in a time of troubles are passengers on a ship caught in a storm when the rigging comes crashing down and must be cut loose. The sails which must be sacrificed are but "folds of dead faith," empty superstructures without living substance. After the removal of enclosures and boundary-stones, new grass can grow. The new men expect "great doctrinal invasions," new ideologies which will keep "the peoples on an angle." There is, at the difficult dawn of a new age, no room for escapist dilettantism: "if the man of talent prefers the rose-garden and the playing of the harpsichord, he shall be devoured by the dogs."

The musical metaphor underlines the contrast with the third speaker, the poet. He is presented as the perpetual rebel and heretic, singing from the hymnbook of the winds, while the Master of song, the god of the winds, "exults at the keyboard of the passions." The poet's song is a celebration of the passionate energies which will carry man to the shores of the future. The winds remove all enclosures, they re-create the unity of Being expressed by the "immense circle of the earth," "the cry of all men," the "entire world of things." Canto VI concludes with images which link the fertility of nature with the cycles of history and, on a larger scale, with the evolution of life through the ages until the very end of time. I consider the last verses of this canto as one of the most striking visions of death ever presented in poetry. The power of this vision is due, I believe, to the several levels on which death occurs and to the richness and concentration of the imagery. The iron helmet where time builds its nest suggests the end of an empire and the arrest of historical time. The three leaves dancing their last dance round a dead Queen's knucklebone express the vanity of all life. From the perspective of eternity, man and nature are but childish toys and their actions but childish games. In the final verse, the "point of dead water and oblivion" recalls the "Dead Seas" of *Anabasis*, the end of the human march. And yet, the nest in the iron helmet or the dance of the leaves round a dead Queen's knucklebone also imply the continuing presence of a vital energy. The "point of dead waters and oblivion" is also "a place of asylum and amber, where the limpid Ocean adds lustre to its grasses, golden amid sacred oils—and the Poet keeps his eyes on purer laminariae," on the precious algae which preserve through eternity the pure essence of life.

Canto VII, the last in the first section of the poem, opens like the fifth canto, with an invocation to Eâ, god of the oceanic depths, who seems to represent the abyss of time. In those intervals when the god of the winds seems to fail, the temptations of doubt must be exorcised. The effort of the spirit to triumph over the weakness of mortal flesh is expressed in a series of metaphors which culminates with the savage swarms of love striving to maintain the height of their flight. The "solicitations of doubt" and the awareness of death must not lead to despair. The Wind shall return to call for another youth fated for battle. Generations of men have passed "along man's road,/Going where men go, to their graves." The voyage west ends in death, but this should be no cause for sadness since the epic march of human history is accompanied by the "lofty narrations of space, still in this wake of splendour westward," where glorious visions hold the symbolic promise of rebirth. As in the great ceremonies where a black horse is sacrificed, death is but a prelude to the divine epiphany of life.

II   Book II. The Quest for Divine Revelation

In the first canto, the promised epiphany appears to have taken place. The discovery of America serves as a metaphor for the gift of a new world, for the birth of a new civilization, for the renewal of fertility, for the return of the sacred, for poetic revelation. Every element of the American scene seems to be overflowing with the primal energy of life. Once again, the archetypal symbol of the wave expresses the poet's faith in the unfailing flow of the cosmic force. In the second canto, the westward movement continues, but winter comes. Stone and metal symbols suggest the arrest of life, the stasis which threatens the forward flow of time. In the iron grip of winter, the American continent appears strewn with the relics of past civilizations, with the dead remains of creatures which once were alive. It would indeed seem that the continuity of life has been broken. Winter can only bring forth "stone fruits" or "brass insects." Other images, however, suggest the emergence of new waters, the return of the divine fire, the *hieros gamos* of Heaven and Earth, the revelation of a new knowledge. But at the threshold of this "great bronze country" where the poet questions the Power which must answer the claim of men, the only answer he receives is silence. He must seek further for the "forcing-places of the wind."

In canto III, the poet's quest takes him South, in the wake of migrating birds. The fact that his march no longer takes him westward may indicate that he has gone astray. The decadent South is apparently used to illustrate the ever-present threat of decay and death. Here again the relics of the past must be exorcised so that a new future may come into being. A symbolic analogy links the march of history, the geological process of erosion, the relentless flow of rivers and the biblical Flood. The waters marching to the open sea carry away "the dead works of this century," but they also follow the progress of a new creation, the new song born amid the corpses of the dead works.

In the following canto, the alluvial islands which the floods have torn away from the river-banks are, in a sense, the analogue of the dead works which swollen rivers carry off to the open sea. They are also "sacred mounds," carrying a burden of new life. They drift down the rivers, guided by the Fates toward the green water of the open sea or destined to be stranded on mudflats. In the conflict between the symbols of decay and death ("anthrax and sanies") and the symbols of generation ("great placentary pouches"), the forces of life seem to prevail. Swarms of bees leave the security of the hive, and eels worm their way into the river-banks. In the rapture of living, all thought of death is forgotten. In the inexhaustible profusion of life, little thought is given to failures or losses. An implicit comparison is made between the history of life on earth and lost fragments of the Bible. In the sacred book of life, page after page has been lost, but new pages are still being written. The Old South is dead, but this "red and gold land of creation" has not been deserted by the divine Power. It reveals itself to the poet-voyager drunk with the sacred drunkenness of mantic revelation. He must now spurn the sweetness of a doomed past, the diseased remnants of a once proud civilization, and heed once more the call of the west winds.

The conflict between the seduction of the South and the call of the West is presented, in canto V, as related to the absence or the presence of the spirit of life. In the first part of the canto, the promised creation has not taken place. The South appears fated to disease and sterility. The Wind no longer blows, the Emissary of

the god has failed in his divine mission, darkness and death celebrate their ominous rituals. In the second part, the sleeper awakes
from the drug-like spell of the South: the Eagle over his head
comes as a warning of the god, and the Wind strengthens the "red
torch of awakening." The Voyager leaves behind the slimy river,
heavy and deep in its bed, the feminine Southland and its paralyzing sweetness. The westward flight, to the whistling of wing and
metal, initiates a new quest. The American West is the spiritual
opposite of the South. It is a land of stone and bone, a hard land,
a dry land. In its narrow gorges, the dead valleys awaken, "with
great cries awaken and smoke again on their shamans' beds," thus
suggesting that the rivers of time have resumed their flow. The
ascetic rule, the difficult march to the heights and the suffering
which it entails are the price to be paid for the anticipated
epiphany. The canto concludes with the heraldic eagle arising in
the wind, soaring over the high mesas where horsemen raise up
the dust from the pottery of dead men and the rose-colored skeletons of sheep.

The theme of life rising from death reintroduced by this symbol
is developed in the last canto of Book II along several parallel
lines. There is, first of all, the march westward which brings to
man the vision of a new landscape. On the far ridges, man sees
the projected reflection of his future. He reads the face of the
earth as a prophetic text and listens to the "bones of a new age of
the Earth." The Voyager thus assumes the role of the poet-shaman.
He presents himself as a receiving apparatus ("texts received in
clear language") which is unable to preserve the purity of the
message in the transmission. The poet is "man assailed by the
god," but "speaking in the equivocal," possibly because human
limitations cannot sustain the assault of mantic revelation. The
insistence on duality echoes other oppositions: between spirit and
flesh, between fire and ashes, between passion and reason. The
"Sun from below," holding its "puma's eye in all this conglomerate
of precious stones," recalls the "occult eye" of "men assailed by the
gods" rather than the "clear eye, in which the man of reason
placed his trust." The black Sun which enables man to decipher
the "new writings" on the "layered pages of great schists" is not
the disabling light of logic, but the illumination of poetry. Another analogy is suggested between the dark energy of the atom
hidden in the heart of matter and the Dionysiac powers at work

within the passionate heart of man. The canto ends as did Book I: men pass on, and their shadows, but the promise remains, in the West, of "forms marching on the peaks, amid the blindness of things," of figures "on the brow of tall limestones, dazzled with presence," of generations of men with new faces ascending toward the summits of the future.

III   Book III. To the Frontiers of the Human

In the first three cantos, Saint-John Perse lists the various categories of men who, through history, have held their faces to the wind. The navigators, the explorers or the conquistadores who discovered and conquered America were, in a literal sense, pushing back the frontiers of the known world. In the second canto, it becomes evident that the discovery of America serves as a symbol for the extension of the human experience. Some conquerors dreamed only of extending their power: soldiers of fortune, in quest of gold and grants, or papal envoys and Puritans bent on bringing the new continent under their law. But others were the "great Protestors," the "dissenters and rebels" who turned America from a land of exile into a place of refuge. Among them, Saint-John Perse lists the followers of bizarre cults, such as mesmerists or snake-worshipers, or the men without purpose who converse with "the grey squirrel and the tree-frog, the animal without halter and the tree without use." Such men decline the charge of "shaking the future in its iron pods." They do not make history, but their presence must not be discounted, since they contribute so much to make man what he is.

The last to appear are the men of science, "readers of pure cartouches in the drums of stone." They do not seek for the empty "placers where lie the scales of a beautiful dream," but for copper or virgin gold, for oil or naphtha, for graphite and uranium, for the "golden midnight wherein to brandish the pirate's torch." The prophets and the seers are not, as in former times, the "adventurers of the soul," the dreamers and the visionaries, they are the explorers of matter, the scientists. The time has come when men will hold in their hands not only the energy of the atom, but the secret of life itself. The excitement and the fear of impending discovery are conveyed in a series of powerful images at the end of canto II.

In the third canto, research scientists appear as the modern equivalent of the "blazers of trails westward." The discoveries which place into human hands the control of nuclear energy are compared to the rape of matter, to "winter nuptials in the fire of the spirit's words, in the fire of great black-diamond roses." But matter blazes with "wild asses" as well as with "virgins." Man has unleashed forces which he may prove powerless to control. In the verse, "May his face inflame the worst scandal of history," we may read an allusion to the bombing of Hiroshima, or, more generally, to the dehumanizing use of science. Driven by their demonic hunger for knowledge, men seek the ultimate secrets of being "in the diagrams of stone and the atom's indices;/At the great forbidden tables where the signs more swiftly pass; in the distant mirrors where the face of the Wanderer passes by. . . ."

The final verse of canto III presents man at the end of his quest. He has become the "exterminator," a "supreme Being" contemplating "the seal of his power, face to face, like a great golden marigold in the hands of the Officiator." Saint-John Perse may have intended the reader to be reminded of the *colchique d'or* or the *herbe d'or* promised in an earlier vision, but there is a significant difference between the golden grass contemplated by the Poet (I,6) and the *souci d'or* held by the Exterminator. The Poet had formed a wish: "let some powerful movement carry us to our limits, and beyond our limits" (I, 6). His wish has been answered, but its fulfilment threatens to bring about the destruction of life itself.

In the first three cantos of Book III, Saint-John Perse thus presents a catalogue of the ways in which men have confronted the wind, of the ways they found of living and climbing. What, then, is man's future? The prophetic ending of Book II gave no answer. It merely asserted that "more than one mask is forming on the brows of tall tall limestones," that there would be a future for man, and that it might assume different forms. When man himself is in question, which is the answer to be chosen? Which is the voice to be heard? In the juncture, "the Poet himself comes out of his millennial rooms . . . with his tribe of attendants," the creatures and the men who, in one way or another, through the ages, have contributed to define the "human presence." The enumeration which follows makes up the major part of canto IV. Reminiscent of similar listings in *Anabasis* or *Exile*, it illustrates not only the infinite variety and plasticity of *la ressource humaine*, but also the compassion, the gentleness, and the solidarity which men have felt for one another. All of these men deserve to be welcomed "at the gangway of the Century," "on the causeway of men," as the wind bends the new grass a hundred leagues away. Saint-John Perse thus implies that there is no real break in the history of mankind, that the winds of renewal will spare the men boarding the ark of time: *"Car c'est de l'homme qu'il s'agit, et de son renouement."* The word seems to refer to the unification of all mankind, both in space and in time, to the creation of a bond between the past and the future as well as between all men on earth.

In cantos V and VI, the Poet speaks. Once again, the great "adventurers of the soul" apply for "precedence on the causeway of men." The men of science must yield to the men of poetry. As they interrogate the earth to know the "meaning of this great disorder," the "adventurers of the soul" may grow "angry at finding no answer": they must not give way to sadness and despair. The destiny of mankind will not be revealed by the disabling logic in which rational man mistakenly placed his trust. If man has lost his way, he will not find it again through the "clear eye" of reason. He must allow himself to be guided by the mysterious forces which Saint-John Perse, through the imagery, associates with lightning, with the sudden onslaught of the "nether god," with the "black Sun from below," with the dark forces of instinct. The Poet appears as the celebrant in dawn ceremonies, ready to receive and retransmit the sacred message. He is man "infested with dream, man overtaken by the divine infection." His drunkenness is that of mantic possession, not to be confused with the psychedelic effects of hemp, belladonna, henbane, or other hallucinogenic plants. The Poet is the medium through whom the "piercing cry of the god" will at last be heard among men. The dots which conclude the canto suggest the impossibility of expressing in human words the unspeakable revelation which has taken place.

IV   Book IV. Return from the Frontier

The narrative resumes at a later time. Deserted by the god, the Poet wonders: "Is there nothing but the human thing?" The silence of the winds leaves him unable to speak, abandoned by the mantic force, cut off from the cosmic flow of life, faced with "the immense emphasis of death, like a great yellow tree before us." If living is this alternate rising and falling, then man must seize upon the surging wave and force it to its limit. This choice is not founded on logic. The poet has no arguments to counter those who laugh and deride the human condition, who seek the protection of illusion or who take refuge in the flesh of woman, in a regressive effort to follow the "wailing river" of time back toward the shelter of infancy. He simply presents another model: the rider who rests his "brow against the saddle at the brief moment of girthing" before resuming the difficult ascent toward the mountain passes. And yet, the insistent question remains: "is there nothing else, is there nothing else but the human thing?"

In the remaining part of the first canto, man appears, as he does in *Exile*, as a Traveler unable to choose between the "monsters" of his fables and the "tender companions" of his nights. The imagery suggests not only the burning intensity of man's fascination with the monstrous unknown, but also its possible vanity. In their obsession with the message of the wind, men refuse the gift of sons to women. They deny the women's grandeur as bearers of life, but to no apparent purpose, since their thoughts keep "their watch-fires along barren shores." Similarly, how vain it seems, "in the great remoteness of things to espy that thundering, always, of great waters advancing toward their Zambezi-lands!" The destructive power of man's obsession with the unknown expressed by the thundering waters reappears in another symbolic form in the next verse, as the hydras defeated by the "bridal arms" of women. Within the framework of this canto, women are presented as the faithful keepers of human values. Faced with the choice between the monstrousness of the beyond and the "ardent history of living creatures," the Traveler that is man resumes once again his journey along the "road of human beings" in pursuit of an answer to the riddle of man's fate.

The geographical exploration described in canto II is also a search for the "new faces" assumed by man in march through space and time. The very purpose of the quest now comes into question. Is there any answer to be found in the "high nameless country, illuminated with horror and void of all sense," among the age-old cultures of the Andes, or still further, on other slopes, on other shores, on the sea? Is life anything more than the meaningless repetition of what has already been lived? Is the history of man as insubstantial as "the signs the moving shadow of the

leaves retraces on the walls everywhere," which are the mere re-
duplication of signs already traced? The leaves reintroduce the
motif of the tree: they suggest the continuity of life, but also its
cyclical nature, the periodic interruptions and repetitions which
scan its becoming. The sea in the West is, again, a sea "familiar to
all our phantoms." The quest goes on, past the first solitary islands, past the volcanic islands (such as Easter Island) with their
"great averted figures" and "long disdainful lips," past the "invio-
late reefs," past the island where, twenty years ago, a last trace of
life still managed to survive, a mere shrub whose identity is uncertain, till there is nothing but the empty expanse of the sea. The
conclusion of the canto expresses in a powerful symbol the possible fate of mankind. The shadow which man projects may one
day cease to mark his course, to trace his history on the sea of
time. Like the unknown shrub on the last island, man may become extinct.

The third canto marks a dramatic reversal in the poet's contemplation. The spirit of man cannot accept the prospect of its own
annihilation. A sudden flash of lightning stops him on the edge of
the nonhuman and causes him to turn back. The Traveler riding
on the causeway of men finds his way blocked by a scar-faced
Stranger arisen from the ditch who causes his horse to shy and
rear and who wrenches the horse's head around to the East.
"What were you going to abandon there?": the Stranger's words
are a call to order. They force the Traveler to regain control of
his horse. The rearing animal appears as a symbol of man's
"scabrous soul," of the wild energy which drives him beyond the
frontiers of the human and threatens to destroy him. The scar-
faced Stranger recalls those men "transfixed by lightning" or put
by lightning in "the path of veracious dreams" who bring salvation to other men, "in wisdom and in vehemence" (I, 6; III, 5).

The fourth canto opens with the contemplated return of the
Traveler to his native land. He will travel by plane, and on the
metal wing a green signal light will be turned on at dusk. In his
vision, the flashing green light becomes a "star of green fire," there
is a "gushing forth of green sap," and the sudden appearance of
the "clear and tender land of our daughters, a golden knife in its
heart!" Nightfall, a green star, vegetation, woman and death: an
identical symbolic cluster was to be found in *Anabasis*, after the
march through the desert. The threat of death is powerless against

the green star which brings to the daughters of men the seeds of a
new life. Other images stress the motif of regeneration and rebirth
in a land still ruled by Mars, the god of war, where the warriors'
beds will remain empty for a long time to come. France at the end
of World War II serves as a symbol for the end of an age, for the
troubled times when a civilization has lost its material goods and
when its spiritual values have been found bankrupt. In his war-
torn country, the returning Traveler appears as the Emissary from
other regions, carrying a "slip of fire in his iron poppy," "new
seeds" for the land, "new vines" for the valleys. Men who go to the
frontiers of the human do not return empty-handed: they bring
back the message of the Wind. Among the "men of the number
and the mass," their mission is to be a thorn in the flesh, the "very
point of the spirit's sword": "The bee of language is on their
brow,/And on the heavy human phrase, kneaded with so many
idioms, they are the only ones to wield the sling of the accent."
Thorn, point, sting, sling: the role of the poet is to disturb, to
attack, to force the "unburied dead" to become alive again. The
poet has seen the City "high under the thunderbolt," and "the
paired prophetic horns still searching the brow of the crowd." The
final verse of the canto offers an explanation of this vision: "such
signs are memorable—like the fork of destiny on the brow of fas-
tidious beasts. . . ." Under the storm, the modern City appears as
a prophetic image. The "golgotha of scrap iron and garbage"
under the "poisonous tree of the sky" (I,6) now appears as a "City
of giant organs under the lightning, as though branched with pure
luminous boughs." Its crowds may be "the number and the mass,"
but the thunderbolt about to strike is now a sign of divine election
and spiritual illumination, not the signal of impending destruction.

Canto V follows a similar pattern. It opens with the harsh in-
dictment of an age which had renounced the spirit of the Wind.
France under the Third Republic becomes the symbol of a decaying civilization which must be rejected so that life may be restored. She perished from an excess of prudence, from the superannuated wisdom and lack of vision so strikingly represented by
stone medallions as blind as blind men's eyes on the façades of the
Halls of Archives. Saint-John Perse aims his most cutting sarcasms
at the symbols of petty bourgeois values venerated by the political
elite of the Third Republic, by the "men of lanes and blind alleys"

who governed France in the twenties and the thirties. The damning inventory is summed up as so much "milk for the gums of the aesthete and for the bulb of the narcissus." The narcissistic complacency and the moral stagnation fostered by the attachment to decaying values are vividly depicted by the "mire of dead leaves in Apollo's basin," in the Versailles gardens. New waters must sluice out the "sediment of the ages," the "garbage and mucus of the past," the "manures" and the "tartars" deposited by a culture which has reached senility.

Triumph over the decomposing past is linked with various manifestations of energy: the rush of new waters, the conquering pleasure of young animals and men in arms splashing through a torrent, like Alexander's cavalry at Arbela, the "black Angel of the lavas" singing his song of "volcanic tromps," the spouting forth of the tallest wave at the passage of the bar. The final victory may not be won. Such images as the "Chouan rising on our woods," an "outbreak of Jacqueries" or a south wind arising "as a backfire" suggest reactionary efforts to delay the birth of a new world. This resistance will only provide "yeast of strength and ferment of soul." Between the squares of the cities where the styles of the past are dying and the "slopes where the future vibrates," the poet's choice is made. The dominant motifs, in the concluding song of the Wind, express his faith in the rebirth of men. The rising sap and the flanks of women are clear symbols of generation. The sharpened splinter of quartz or obsidian has the penetrating thrust of a weapon. The watchtowers which are the poet's thoughts suggest his prophetic vision. The "abyss of his eyes" reveals the future which will be shaped by his dreams. Men will "weave the gesture" into the "braid of his song": their actions will be inspired by his visions and turn them into realities.

The last two cantos sum up the main themes of the poem. If the great winds blowing over the land of men sing the "horror of living," they also proclaim the "honour of living." The great forces at work on the "causeway of men" lead the new men to their new ways, free them from the chains of the past. The earth is stripped bare "on the savage stone of misfortune," but only to be offered for "new nuptials" to the new men. Other images suggest the cyclical progress of man through history, the alternation of war and peace, of death and renewal, of spiritual exile and mantic revelation. There are waves which lift men to the very summit of the instant and cast them onto new shores. There is the swimmer who, standing on the beach, still feels inhabited and propelled by the "helix of being," by the intoxicating memory of the wind. Significant motifs are linked together in a typical cluster: the world visited by a new bee, the burning of white clay as it cleaves to the tongue, the storm which refreshes, the live force, the bed newly made, the linen purified from a fetid smell, the face recovered from the gods, things reborn among the debris of wing-sheaths and shells, the fire burning again in the forges, the swords beaten into plowshares, the earth moving under the plow like a woman loved by a man.

The theme of divine visitation is taken up once again with the question: "Will the gods, taken with drink, venture again on the earth of men?" The poet answers in the affirmative. Divine messengers will come again to the daughters of the earth and give them children, a new race of men will be born to the daughters of his race, his poems will bear seed and fruit among men of another age, and his living cry will echo along the causeway of men, from place to place and from man to man. Saint-John Perse thus proclaims his faith in the eternity of being, in the unity and immortality of the human race, in the endless revelation of poetry. The final canto is a brief parable. The very old tree described at the beginning of the poem has survived the violent assault of the winds. Although barren of leaves, it has resumed the drivelling "thread of its maxims." Another tree of high degree is "already rising from the great subterranean Indies,/With its magnetic leaf and its burden of new fruits." The sterile wisdom of the past would still preach its useless message at the dawn of a new age, but a new world has already begun to displace a world in its dotage.

V   *The Power of Plurisignation*

Winds appears as a complex structure made up of multiple superimposed and related levels. It is the poet's *summa*, the conscious synthesis of his dominant motifs which are brought together and developed along parallel lines within a single work. In a literal sense, the winds are a natural phenomenon, a powerful cosmic force. They blow across the surface of the earth, scattering the dust of past seasons and bringing new seeds to a worn out soil.

The winds are also the forces which, since time immemorial, drove men westward. Those are the winds which brought an end to the Roman Empire, and, later, to medieval Europe. The Barbarian invaders who sacked Rome and the men who discovered America listened to their call. They were explorers, conquerors, reformers, adventurers and dreamers. They were men of the frontier, forever reaching beyond the boundaries of the known world. The theme of geographical exploration is thus linked to the theme of historical becoming. Ancient civilizations decay and die. The winds are the forces of historical violence, of the revolutions and wars which are instruments of renewal and change. In Saint-John Perse's cosmogony, the cyclical succession of death and rebirth is the dominant principle. This is probably why he borrowed the symbol of the Cosmic Tree from ancient Indo-European mythologies. The winds are those powers which seem to threaten total destruction, but which actually mark the beginning of a new cosmic cycle. Saint-John Perse thus raises to the mythic level the advent of the nuclear age. In the age-old myths concerned with the Eternal Return, with cosmic cycles which end in apocalyptic conflagrations followed by new creations, the poet finds a message of hope.

Next to *Seamarks, Winds* is Saint-John Perse's longest poem. It comprises four books. The first and the last consist of seven cantos, the second and third of six cantos. The symmetry of this design, reinforced by echoing verses and parallel images, underlines its circular structure and emphasizes the cyclical nature of the fundamental theme: the poet's abiding faith that man will emerge triumphant from his darkest hours. This optimism may bear some relation to the historical conjuncture at the time when the poem was written. World War II had just come to an end. The civilization which had been the pride of ancient Europe had proved unable to prevent a disaster of such magnitude. Mankind faced the prospect of its own annihilation and stood on the threshold of a new age. The poet himself had overcome the sadness and the nostalgia of his exile. Rejecting any sterile regret for the paralyzing blandishments of the past, he welcomed a new world free at last from the narrow wisdom, the timid cautiousness and the petty selfishness so often typical of the French bourgeoisie since the reign of Louis-Philippe.

VI *The Poet's Itinerary*

The spiritual drama which unfolds in the poetry of Saint-John Perse reaches its resolution in *Winds*. In this drama, which has been masterfully analyzed by Claude Vigée, *Snows* marks the "phase of askesis," the "moment of disincarnation." [3] In *Snows*, more than in any other poem of *Exile*, renunciation of anything human has been carried to its extreme point. *Snows* expresses the spirit's ultimate efforts not only to renounce its own humanity, but to find in the purity of nothingness the very essence of Being. It must be clear, however, that *Snows* represents but one moment in the poet's dialectic to be negated at the next moment. This pattern of alternation is a characteristic feature in the poetry of Saint-John Perse. The sea of *To Celebrate a Childhood* is "haunted by invisible departures," but the planter of *Written on the Door* feels no envy for the passing ships. The warriors of *Anabasis* dream of settling down in their maritime provinces, amid their perfumed daughters: they soon resume their march across the desert sands. As for the Princes of *Exile*, there can be no end to their flight along the barren shores. They will not fall prey to the "equivocal eagle of happiness." In *Rains*, he who "drinks of divinity," but whose "mask is made of clay," is equally divided.

A similar conflict takes place in *Winds*. It reaches a climax in the spiritual illumination which occurs at the crucial moment when the soul reaches the limits of human experience. Faced with its own dissolution in the nonhuman, the spirit experiences a deep reversal and returns to the world which it had renounced. Its itinerary, as Gabriel Bounoure remarks, is equally the inverse itinerary: "The world cannot be apprehended in its eternal, poetic life except at the price of a detour through emptiness. . . . And when the two trajectories, to the silence of the ode, end by being one, then the operation of poetry is accomplished, at once magic and mystic." [4] The wind is that power in man which will not allow him to be satisfied with what is. The wind is that force which lifts man and carries him forward, then leaves him with the memory of his lost greatness, with the dreams he dared to dream, with the vision which transcends all human wisdom. The wind is the voice of revelation speaking through the poet who has become its instrument. The function of the poet, in the society of men, is to welcome the voice which comes from the unknown, from the empty space which lies beyond the real, to heed the lightning which strikes on the frontiers of the soul and will guide mankind to the shores of divinity.

The Epic of Mankind   107

welcome the voice which comes from the unknown, from the
empty space which has been enriched, to heed the lightning
which strikes on the frontiers of the soul and will guide mankind
to the shores of divinity.

CHAPTER 6

The Quest for Divinity

THE publication of *Seamarks,* in 1957, was hailed as a major
literary event. This masterpiece of Saint-John Perse's mature
years had been nearly ten years in the making. The first fragment
appeared in 1948. Other parts were to follow during the succeeding years, so that by 1956 the totality of the poem was already
known to the reading public. These fragments, however, did not
acquire their full meaning until they were fitted into the architecture of the completed poem. In a work of these dimensions (one
hundred and eighty pages in the American edition), the formal
design apparent in the final text emphasized its essential unity. In
an explanatory letter, Saint-John Perse has stressed the significance of this formal structure.[1]

I *The Thematic Structure of* Seamarks

Saint-John Perse compares *Seamarks* to the ritual dramas per-
formed at ancient Greek festivals in honor of the gods. This does
not mean that the formal structure of the poem actually follows
the pattern of a Greek tragedy. *Seamarks* has probably more in
common with the dithyramb, a choral lyric sung by a circular
choir. It is also quite possible that Saint-John Perse found his
major inspiration in the physical design of the Greek theater,
which appears to have been originally intended for the performance of dithyrambs. The center was the orchestra, or "dancing
place," a circular space. The altar of the god stood in the middle.
The chorus was disposed around the altar. In *Seamarks,* the sea is
the divinity to be honored. It may therefore be identified with
the "solitary arena" and the "ritual center," with "the altar table of
ancient drama, around which the drama unfolds, and around
which the secondary figures or the main protagonists first take
their places, like fragments of mankind representing the age-old

earth of men, forever brought into question." A similar design is evoked in the poem itself, which is presented as a "Poetry to accompany the march of a recitation in honour of the Sea./Poetry to assist the song of a march round the circuit of the Sea./Like the ritual round the altar and the gravitation of the chorus in the circuit of the strophe" (*Invocation,* 3). The word strophe, which is also the title of the second part, is taken here in its etymological sense of "evolution of the chorus around the altar." It has been noted that "*Seamarks,* as a poem celebrating the sea, includes within itself the recitation of a ritual having the same purpose of celebrating the sea. There are thus three dimensions to account for, the sea, the rite, the poem." [2] All three dimensions are clearly indicated in the author's own comments on the structure of the poem.

The first part (*Invocation*) introduces the main theme: the Poet's recourse to the Sea as "the source of all animation and re-creation." In the heart of men, the Sea is that presence which inspires and assists, which provides help, mediation, and revelation. The march around the Sea, like the procession around the altar, is a ritual preparation for the intercession of the Sea, for the generation of the poem. The second part (*Strophe*) introduces the eight figures or groups called upon to represent the diverse reactions of men faced with the Sea: questioning, entreaty, imprecation, initiation, appeal, or celebration. In the third part (*Chorus*), all this "human exaltation in honor of the Sea" is gathered together in a single collective voice. Man enters into communion with the Sea, which is identified as the source of power and knowledge, as Universal Being. The French title of the poem, *Amers,* refers not only to the bitter salt waters of the sea but also to the landmarks on the shore. This second meaning, which suggests the meeting of two elements—earth and water, land and sea —seems to express the encounter of two worlds, the human and the divine. This experience is perceived as a transgression, as a perilous quest which the Poet undertakes "for higher celebrations of the spirit and graver spiritual adventures." The collective recitation finally gives way to a vast procession of men and women led by the Poet who, in his capacity as Master of the Chorus, guides the entire population of the City toward the Sea, "image of a humanity marching toward its highest destiny." In the final section

(*Dedication*), the Poet's task is completed. He is now free to divest himself of the ritual mask which he wore for the ceremony described in the poem.

This account of *Seamarks* by the author provides further justification for the comparison with ancient Greek drama. The confrontation between the human and the sacred lies at the heart of Greek tragedy. The mystery which encompasses the human condition is made perceptible to the audience. A similar confrontation takes place in *Seamarks* between the City of men and the divine Sea. It finds its culmination and its resolution in the ritual union between a virgin of the City and a man from the Sea. The ritual entry of the procession into the Sea and the consumption of the god in his holiest species also suggest the integration of the human and the divine (*Chorus,* 2). The ritual described in *Seamarks* may thus be linked to three sacramental acts: marriage, baptism and communion. All three are epiphanies: they call for the manifestation of a divine presence. Since the poem itself is presented as part of the ritual, it must have an identical purpose. The symbolic recreation of divine revelation is a means of ensuring its return. The language miming the experience brings about its repetition. The poem itself is a ritual.

II *Invocation*

The first canto opens with a question from an unidentified speaker who can only be the poet himself or his persona. He speaks for the population of the City assembled along the Sea. The Sea thus appears as a living opposite to the "ode of stone" which surrounds it. Its withdrawal would deprive the City of all living energy, but the prospect is raised only to underscore its utter impossibility. The imagery stresses the proximity of the Sea, in space and in time. The Sea is "our vigil." The word has been carefully chosen for its dual meaning. The Sea is a sentinel at the frontiers of mankind. It is also the eve which precedes a feast day, the "dawn to the orient of men," the festive promise of an "age without decline," of a "divine promulgation." The word feast recurs seven times in the opening canto, emphasizing the religious tone suggested by the image of "the Sea as celebrated in our dreams, like an Easter of green grasses." The Sea symbolizes the coming of a new day, the birth of the future, the carefree squandering of an inexhaustible force. The fear of death and nothingness is dispelled by the breeze blowing from the open sea, which comes as a flood leading to a new birth.

In the second canto, the poet assumes a new identity: he is a man of the sea, the "Singer of the most beautiful song," and his song will bring joy and delight to men "seated under the great tree of sorrow." It will lead them "among the ferns again of childhood," when the "unrolling fronds of death" did not hold them under its paralyzing spell. The song of the sea will restore the "carefreeness of death" which is the privilege of the child. The ritual evolution of the chorus is presented in the third canto as a propitiating act intended to bring about the birth of this song. Poetic creation is the manifestation, within the heart of man, of a divine presence, an unexpected gift. Through the similarity of sound, the French word *aubaine,* which means godsend, good fortune, also carries connotations of the freshness of dawn, of an alien origin, and of a sacred ceremony. Poetic creation partakes of the wild energy of the Sea, of the holy secrets which it may reveal "in the overflowing of its bubbles and the infused wisdom of its milk . . . like a Sibyl in flower on her iron chair. . . ." *Seamarks* thus appears firmly rooted in a symbolic vision of the sea which may be traced back to the most primitive cosmogonies. The sea is the primeval substance from which all life proceeds, the sacred principle which ensures its perenniality. The subject of the poem, as it is defined in the fourth canto, is not the sea itself, but its "reign in the heart of man," its mythical image. In his celebration of the Sea, the poet sees himself as a courtier who, in presenting his plea to the Prince, must observe the minutiae of the prescribed ritual (*Invocation,* 4).

In the fifth canto, the poet abandons for a moment his persona: he is no longer the Singer of the ritual chant, but the author of *Seamarks.* Saint-John Perse thus emphasizes the opposition between the poet's everyday personality, busy with his daily routine, and his secret self who for so long "nursed a taste for this poem." The poet may present the same appearance as other men, but he speaks the "tongue of an alien." Poetic revelation is expressed through a series of metaphors which suggest the manifestation of a divine Being. The Sea is the poet's morganatic spouse, his "far off Bride." In his daily talk, he mingles "all that alliance, afar, of a great flash of sea . . . vivid scale, among the meshes, of a great fish taken by the gills!" The capture of a sea creature is also implied by the comparison of the poem to Halley's comets, "the beautiful celestial visitors in Vestal robes, caught in the night by the hook of glass," but so "prompt to escape at the turn of the ellipse."

In another verse, poetic inspiration is linked to the rising tide and to the surging power of the unconscious. The poet is invaded by the great poem as by "the milk of madrepores," in a very slow heaving of the "great waters of dream." Through this poem, which may be his last work ("My last song! my last song!"), he will declare his allegiance to the Sea. The poem will be a monument in her honor comparable to Aliscamps or the Propylaeas. At the end of the canto, the poet no longer speaks in his own name. He is no longer the author of *Seamarks*, but a man commissioned by an Assembly of Donors to prepare the text and the announcement for the ceremonial foundation of a great votive work. He thus resumes the ritual role of the Narrator who will recite the ceremonial poem of mankind to the Sea. In this "nuptial chant" which consecrates man's alliance with the Sea, "She, such an Alien," comes to mirror herself.

A similar metaphor appears in the final canto of the *Invocation*. The Sea which "came to us on the stone steps of the drama" becomes the "Recitation marching towards the Author and towards the painted mouth of his mask." The Sea stands as a clear symbol for the mythopoeic powers of poetic imagination as she brings to the poet "all her breed of immortal fables." The Sea is the language of poetry "running to its massive splendour of a very fine periodic style," gliding on "its coils of a black python,/Very great thing moving towards the night and towards divine transgression. . . ." Saint-John Perse makes effective use of the traditional symbol of the snake, which carries connotations of eternal becoming, of perennial fertility, of divine revelation.[3] In the dreams of men, the vision of the Sea is the manifestation of a sacred mystery, just as in ancient times a "great tub of entrails and offal" could take the Sacrificer to the limits of the human. This revelation is a form of knowledge free from any conventional code, from any system of interpretation pre-established by men. The Sea is the unmediated presence of Being, "inallusive and innocent of all figures." This experience, which carries man beyond all human limits, is presented as the sacred marriage of a man and an immortal. The ecstasy of poetic revelation brings to man the "Sea with the scent of female entrails and of phosphorus, in the great cracking whips of rape." The poem is born when the human spirit seizes the Sea "in the fire of [its] finest acts," in "that pure instant of equity" which makes of man the equal of a god.

The *Invocation* ends with two parallel series of corresponding symbols in which the "daughters of mortal women" are opposed to the divine Bride, the straying votive lamps carried by the participants in the procession to the flashing flame of cinnabar thrown into the sacred fire, and the light of human wisdom to the illumination of poetic vision. Poetry is that power which restores man to his divine estate, to the "fair land of the King that he has not seen since childhood," to the Edenic unity with the very essence of Being.

III *Strophe*

1. *Tall Cities flamed in the sun all along their sea front* . . . In each of the nine cantos which make up the *Strophe,* the sea appears as a commanding presence, as a compelling call addressed to the world of men. The setting evoked in this title ("a hemicycle of maritime cities, port installations, and rural suburbs") is used to suggest the conflicting attitudes of mankind toward the sea.[4] There have been tall Cities, eager to enter into a pact of alliance with the sea. This union takes the form of a ceremonial wedding, a possible reference to the ritual marriage of Venice and the Adriatic. In *Winds,* a woman was exposed to the night, alone and naked, in order to induce the god to return among men. In *Seamarks,* the woman whose body is the "golden number" forebodes a similar hierogamy. An allusion to the fate of Andromeda, who was chained to a rock as a sacrificial victim to placate a monster from the sea, confirms this interpretation. Perseus, mounted on Pegasus, flew to her rescue. In *Seamarks,* however, Pegasus is not the true bearer of salvation. The powers of poetry are not identified with the "winged beast," with this ambiguous composite of animality and spirituality, but with the Sea itself, which leads "its golden responses, in great luminous phrases and great pangs of green fire." Only the "men of memory," faithful perhaps to a discarded fable, would place their City under the aegis of "some winged beast." The following expresses the City's yearning for another hierogamy: "But the male ring, in the muzzle of the pierheads, under the white feather trophy, dreamed, dreamed, amid

the foam,/Of more distant relays where foam flies from other manes. . . ."

The contrast between the "Tall Cities flaming in the sun" and the "Low-lying Cities" which "prospered in ignorance of the sea" may refer to a symbolic opposition between cities which flourished on the sea trade, such as Tyre, Athens or Venice, and cities with an agricultural past, such as Rome. It is clear, however, that the main opposition is neither historical nor economical, but spiritual in nature. The low-lying Cities turn their backs to the sea. Pollution, disease, and death mark them as symbols of the Waste Land, while the sea restores purity, beauty, and life. The Earth is compared to Circe, the "ancient Sorceress" who turned Ulysses' companions into swine, thus reducing men to their material nature. A caged bird and the tamed eyes of landsmen give further indication that men bound to the earth are deprived of spiritual freedom. The "laughter of the sea" which makes its way to the heartland is a liberating force. As it sets in the west, toward the shipyards, the sun appears as the prophet of a new faith pointing the way to the sea to shepherds and ploughmen. The dark fascination of the sea combines the intoxicating powers of wine and sex, of music and prophecy. The following cantos of the *Strophe* give voice to the responses evoked by the sea in the burning hearts of men.

2. *From the Master of stars and navigation* . . . The first to speak is the Master of stars and navigation. "He reads in the stars the way which the Lord's finger shows us": such was the poet's role, according to Vigny (*Chatterton*, III, 6). Saint-John Perse has not renounced this Romantic concept. The poet is the Seer, watching for the hour when the "secret of the world" is at last revealed to his eyes. He is the Pilot who leads men to the "threshold of knowledge," to the "doorsteps of glory," and who guides them through the boundless expanse of Time. Standing on the "edge of the great waters," he communes with the dark forces which recognize neither limit nor control, with madness and desire, with dream and ecstasy. In the "total Sea," all oppositions are reconciled: past and future, darkness and light, dream and reality, drunkenness and lucidity. The Master of stars and navigation has seen a star break "its chain in the stables of Heaven" and travel "in the heights of the green Century." A parallel image occurs in the comparison of the "prophetic breath" to the "flame of green fire

among the flora of the reef." As he spreads his nets for the night, the Master of stars and navigation hopes to capture the "wandering star," just as in preceding cantos men hoped to capture "beautiful celestial visitors" or the maned creatures of the Sea. In the concluding verses, a similar attempt is made by the "Women who bathe in night, at the ends of islands." The symbolic pattern thus established is repeated in the remaining cantos of the *Strophe*.

3. *The Tragediennes came. . . .* As in the preceding cantos, the Tragediennes pay homage to the Sea and call for the restoration of its alliance. They have come to denounce the degradation of their art, which reflects the decadence of man. Their contemporaries are only "spectres," pitiful shadows of ancient heroes. The spiritual degeneration of the times is revealed in a striking image: "And the golden sandal of the great Tragedians shines in the urine pits of the arena/With the patrician star and the green keys of the setting sun." The Tragediennes are creatures of the earth, but they retain the nostalgia of a "higher language on the shores," the message of the Sea. The nature of their hope is suggested by their propitiatory gift, their own bodies, "this offering of human clay where the expected face of the god is taking shape." In their yearning for the rebirth of greatness, they will even "produce on the sacred shield of the belly the hairy mask of sex." This gesture is compared to the action of Perseus holding up the "severed head of a woman—Stranger or Magician." It appears as a desperate appeal for the restoration of life in a world cut off from the very source of life. The art of their time no longer knows the touch of "divine lips." As they approach the "debased texts" of their century, the Tragediennes' lips feel only reluctance and long for the "living Sea of a greater text," for "great seditious works, great licentious works, open to every audacity of man." Such works express the divine potential of man. They are not bound by narrow poetic codes, by petty literary conventions or definitions. Their lofty style comes "from the sea and farther than the sea," their larger meter will "chain us to that greater narration of things throughout the world, behind all things of the world." The Tragediennes' wishful question defines their aspiration: "To the movement of the princely waters who will again tie for us the great phrase taken from the people?" Through the rhythms of such great texts, the distant movement of the crowd will become one with the rising of the Sea, with the very pulse of Being. Raising

their arms toward the sea, the Tragediennes call for a new Master, for a "man of the gods" who will awake among men the sense of a higher destiny, for the Poet who will restore the "greatness of man on the stone," on the stage upon which he was placed by history.

4. *The Patrician Women also are on the terraces.* . . . For the Patrician Women, as for the Tragediennes, the values which once gave meaning to life are threatened by decay. The disintegration of an aristocratic order is expressed through a series of motifs and symbols: failure, lies, betrayal, scorched gardens, a dead feather, a rose without perfume, a cracked curbstone. Alone and half-naked in their festive garments, the Women have escaped the confining walls of the royal court, the stifling social order which had become for them a place of exile. At the edge of their white terraces overlooking the sea, they stand on the threshold of a new world. The violent motions of women making love or giving birth reflect the violence of the stormy sea. This symbolic association also suggests that the violence of history does not lead to death, but to life. The Sea becomes a "very great rose of alliance and a very great hierarchical tree—like a great tree of expiation at the meeting of invasion roads." Under its awesome burden of death, the living tree bears mute witness to the continuity of life. The Patrician Women are a figure of human hope and desire. They look for their salvation to the "dark marble of the sea" where the "cipher of the gods" is inscribed. They embody the human longing for "the natal place where we were not born," for the "royal place where we have no seat," for the lost Kingdom obscurely remembered as "a country of the future."

5. *Language which was the Poetess.* . . . The speech of the Poetess follows an identical pattern. The discovery of the sea is a spiritual awakening. A spell has been broken. The Poetess, and other women like her, have been freed from the drugged drowsiness which kept them prisoners in "the stable of happiness." As she aspires to the forbidden knowledge which passes all understanding, the Poetess becomes a figure of the human soul yearning for the violent "love of the god equal to invective, the great talons raking [her] woman's flesh." The revelation of the sacred inspires the same fascination as incest, an obscene tumor, or an epileptic seizure. The soul which falls prey to the demonic forces of the self experiences these forces as supernatural manifestations, as "divine

hosts," as "masters of the whip" driving it to the frontiers of the human.

6. *And this girl prophet among the Priests* . . . Mantic possession, like poetic inspiration, is a manifestation of the sacred forces symbolized by the sea. "The girls bound at the foot of the Capes," like Andromeda waiting for the monster, "take the message there." The Girl Prophets cannot repeat the "things not very tellable" and only half-perceived under the foam. Their gagged mouths, devoid of human speech, speak more clearly for "the god they relay." In *Seamarks,* the Sea fulfills the same liberating function as the cosmic energy of *Winds.* The rigid structures of the past are destroyed so that the sacred power of life may pursue its course: "The earth with loosened stones comes to its undoing at the brink of those waters." Men must not be content with the "earthly side of man, blinded by domestic stars." They must not seek to imprison the god within stone sanctuaries, they must not remain the slaves of frozen spiritual forms, but "go forth and grow in stature, rather than build," over the black waters of the future. In its perpetual metamorphosis, nature appears as a promise of immortality. The rain pours "the white oats" of a divine message, just as the manna gave proof of God's favor to the Hebrews wandering through the desert. A flight of small dark birds scattering like "the black salt of a portent," the cry of a sea bird at its highest mating, the Girl Prophets working in the rice swamps, all express the same message: the "continuity of the things to come,/like a holy saliva and like an eternal sap." They all take their place in the "newborn phrase which has no end," in the endless chain of cosmic becoming.

7. *One evening raised by divine hand* . . . The daughters of the earth who follow the girl prophet also proclaim their alliance with the Sea. The last evening of their girlhood has the sweetness of a new dawn. The hour has come when they must leave their mothers' sheltered gardens. They are prepared to assume their role in the unfolding drama of mankind. The violence of history does not lead them to seek refuge in death. They will not imitate the famous widows who escaped humiliation and sorrow through suicide, as did Cleopatra and Dido. As they stand, ready to confront the future, they represent that moment in history when a new generation, or a new civilization, prepares to enter upon the

stage and to challenge the whip and the sword of historical becoming. The adventure of man on earth is also presented as a
dance: a time comes, in the weak moment of the dance, when the
dancer would be overcome by nausea were it not for the entrance
of the chorus, "like the sea itself hammering the mound of its
swell." The chorus, with its horned masks, suggests the sudden appearance of characters dressed as satyrs, the sudden manifestation
of Dionysiac energies, the return of the regenerating Sea. To the
young girls, the gift of the sea is the promise of joyful rebirth, of
immortality. A final cluster of images suggests the eager expectation of the earth for the fecundating power of the sea.

8. *Stranger, whose sail* . . . In ancient societies where sacred
prostitution was practiced, women sold themselves to strangers in
the precincts of temples. This rite is commonly interpreted as re-
producing the union of the great Mother Goddess with her divine
Lover. The Stranger from the sea fulfills a similar function. The
unconscious force which brings about the union of man and
woman does not represent the blind drive of animal instinct. For
Saint-John Perse, erotic ecstasy pertains to the sacred. It is a form
of transgression, the conquest of a forbidden knowledge. The
breeze which blows from the highlands carries with it the taste of
"dead hearths," as "illustrious Ladies, on the capes, [open] to the
fires of the evening a nostril pierced with gold." The question is
asked: "Will the stone hand of destiny be offered us again?" The
Lover from the sea must restore the divine spark to the "custom-
ridden land" and its "dead hearths." In the concluding verses, the
criste-marine, with its "taste of flesh, of all flesh the happiest,"
and the earth "crying out on its porous banks amidst the avid
brambles and live roses/Of the foam" are concrete expressions of
sexual possession, which in turn appears as a symbol of divine
revelation.

9. *Narrow are the vessels* . . . Many critics consider this canto
as Saint-John Perse's masterpiece. They rank it on a par with the
Song of Songs among the highest celebrations of love ever written
by man.[5] Its length equals nearly half of the entire *Strophe*, an
indication of its crucial significance in the framework of the poem.
After the Patrician Women and the Poetess, after the Prophetess
and the daughters of the City, the Lovers are the last called to pay
homage to the sea. Their testimony is a poem within a poem, a
dramatic dialogue in which Man and Woman speak alternately.

Their antiphon (parts 2 to 6) is set between two symmetrical sections in which the leading motifs are introduced and later brought to their conclusion. The central symbol is contained in the opening line of part 1: "Narrow are the vessels, narrow our couch. . . ." The Lovers' bed becomes a ship sailing over the boundless expanse of the sea. In the act of love, man and woman transcend the narrow confines of their humanity. Their embrace is a rite through which they become one with the ceaseless flow of Being: "One same wave throughout the world, one same wave since Troy/Rolls its haunch toward us." The entrance of Summer, the rising of the stars, the coming of dawn, the rhythm and rumor of the sea, all are signs of renewal and rebirth, all promise triumph over decline and decay, victory over sterility and death (part 1).

The Woman is the first to speak. The mounting of desire is described as the rising of the tide. As the Lover undresses her, she sees herself as the vine trampled by the conquering sea, as the shore upon which the man born of the sea lies stretched out, as the spring beneath the sands at which he may refresh his face, as the soil on which he may rejoice, as the fruit of which he may eat. The vision of "tall enraptured girls" which the sea lays down in tears among their loincloths and unbraided tresses reinforces the image of the sea as the male conquering principle. The Woman, however, also bears within herself the essence of the sea. This is precisely what the Man seeks in her: "O my love who tastes of the sea. . . ." Both are, at the same time and for each other, the "female land" and the "salacious, supple sea," both are lifted by the rising "seas of desire." The Woman's body is also the votive vessel sailing against death under its "burden of a man's night." "There is no higher usurpation than in the vessel of love": the Lovers usurp a condition which does not belong to man. Their lovemaking is a theogamy. The "red poppy of the goddess" glistens between the Woman's teeth, while her Lover appears to her as "a god tattooed with male fern." Love is experienced as a form of identification with an alien power. Man becomes the temporary host of a god in animal form, the "falcon of desire," the "salacious Conger of desire." As in the ancient myths of Leda and the Swan, of Europa and the Bull, the combination of animality and divinity emphasizes the irrational, extrahuman origin of the erotic impulse (parts 2 and 3). In the act of love, the Woman's body opens shamelessly to the "Stallion of the rite, like the sea itself to the assaults of the lightning."

La mer, l'amour, la mort: these echoing words suggest a paradoxical analogy between conflicting principles. A further link is created through the symbols of the wave, the snake, and the lightning bolt. The wave is "the Sea raised against death." It is love, marching through time to an encounter with eternity. As "the tall wave curving and sleek on its painted cobra's throat," it becomes identified with death. It is also the overpowering wave which surges and breaks at the climax of erotic pleasure, in that instant when "the very tall comb of immortality" crowns the radiant foam, when a woman haunts the forbidden realm of fable, when the tears she sheds are no longer the tears of a mortal creature. The snake, like the "Stallion of the rite" and the "Royal Conger," is an obvious male symbol, but its meaning extends far beyond its phallic connotations. The Woman also appears as a snake. She is "the Lover, erect in wrath, who recoils, who bends taut, and stands fast," uttering "her hissing of lover and priestess. . . ." The snake is love itself, poised to strike. Finally the snake is death, "sleek on its painted cobra's throat," held in check by the countervailing power of love. Lightning is primarily an erotic symbol, but its capacity to strike like a snake suggests other associations. Male and female, fire and water, life and death, mortal and god, generation and destruction, splendor and sadness: in the ecstasy of love, the reconciliation of opposites is accomplished, all contradictions are resolved, and the human soul merges with the totality of Being.

The union of Man and Woman is a ritual act. It actualizes what it represents, a hierogamy, the interpenetration of the human and the divine, of life and what lies beyond life. The poet is well aware, however, that the "sadness" is already in the "splendour." The epiphany is experienced as already past ("You, god, who were there, my guest, keep alive in me the helix of your rape."), and the triumphant illumination as "the flaming brazier of the shipwreck." The hierogamy which took place is seen as a transgression, as an intrusion into a forbidden kingdom. The Lover is left with an uncertain memory, and the feeling of an irrevocable exile. As a ritual act intended to accomplish the fusion of the human and the divine, love may thus appear powerless. The theme of mimicry expresses this failure: "To haunt the Being is but act of a mime." The efficacy of the rite is thus brought into question, but all doubts are soon rejected in this ringing affirmation: "To haunt the Being is not a delusion. And the Woman who loves is no mime." The symbol *is* the reality. In the act of love, the Woman *is* the "Sibyl open on her rock" to the conquering god, and the god *is* in her cry. She *is* "Ishtar, splendid and naked, spurred with light-ning bolts and green eagles," and her cry rings over the waters (part 4).

For Saint-John Perse, poetry also originates in the alien pres-ence which takes possession of the human soul. The storm at sea, the erotic climax, mantic trance or poetic ecstasy, all are expres-sions of a power which transcends death. Things go to their end, but the course of things has no end. The Lovers' bed becomes a ship gliding through the tropical night. It carries life itself, free at last from the "thorn of fear," from the anguish of death. A central motif runs through the imagery. Everything bears witness to the inexhaustible fecundity of life (part 5). There is no frontier be-tween the "narrow human shore" and the "high free wave that no one harnesses or compels." There is no conflict between the faith-ful Spouse and the "Sea adulteress and sorceress," between the Woman's love and Man's nomadic heart, between the concrete reality of the world and the alien kingdom of the dream. The Lover does not yearn for the eternity of transcendence. He does not seek the absolute in Plato's "ghostly paradigm of things," but in their elemental substance. The wisdom of Homer and Pindar is echoed in his affirmation of immanence: " 'Keep,' said the man in the tale, 'keep, O non-mortal Nymph, your offer of immortality. Your island is not mine where the tree sheds no leaves; neither does your couch move me, where a man does not face his destiny.'/Rather the couch of humans, honoured by death! . . . I will exhaust the road of mortal man . . ." [6]

The Lovers' ship sails toward the high sea. The symbolic mean-ing of their quest is expressed through a recurrent image in the poetry of Saint-John Perse, the swarming of bees. Leaving behind the receding land, its "custom" and its "ease," the bees have set forth toward the "immense hive of the future." The lessons of the past are a useless impediment. The sunset on the horizon is seen as "that chasm of splendour where all the wreckage of history and the painted patterns of dead ages are thrown to oblivion," but the unconscious energy at work in the evolution of life and in the course of history cannot fail to reach its goal. "The gods go naked to their work," "The gods go blinded on the black water," but "Happy those who stray at sea!" The dance of Shiva, the god of destruction and fecundation, symbolizes the endless cycle of death and rebirth: "And from the divine heel, that very strong pulsation which rules everywhere. . . ." As it endures through time, the world is but the manifestation of the "divine veracity," of the unfailing unity and continuity of Being (part 6). In the final part of the canto, winter has replaced summer. In the temporal cycle, the season of death has succeeded the season of life. In the heart of the Lovers, the sea is no longer felt as a triumphant presence. Images of decay, corruption, and death seem to prevail. Another key motif is indicated through the figure of the ship which adorns the City gates, the foreign coins in the shape of a small boat, or the image of the ship nailed on the closed doors of the Lovers: mimicry. Through the ritual of love, the Women, with their eyes "barred by the sea," restore the lost presence and triumph over time. A similar motif appears in the mention of the masks. Through their ritual wearing, men assume the identity of supernatural beings and triumph over death: "Lovers, the sea follows us! Death is not. The gods hail us in the port. And from under our beds we pull our largest family masks." In the economy of *Seamarks*, this concluding verse of the *Strophe* has another function: it reasserts the ritual form of the poem and serves as an introduction to the *Chorus* which follows. Instead of separate groups speaking in succession, the entire population of the City will now speak with a single voice in celebration of the Sea.

IV   *Chorus*

In the five cantos of the *Chorus*, as might be expected, one theme is dominant: in the unity of the Sea, all contradictions are resolved, all oppositions are reconciled. The "Sea of Baal," the god of mountains and storms, the god of the heights, is also the "Sea of Mammon," whom Christian tradition erroneously assumes to be a Syriac deity, the god of earthly goods, the god of the lower parts, and the "Sea of Dagon," the god-fish. The Sea is the divine power which transcends all the particularized forms which men have used to represent the sacred. More generally, the Sea symbolizes the mystery of universal Being which transcends all human distinctions: past and future, reality and dream, reason and

madness. The "Sea without arbiter or council" cannot be sub-
sumed under human categories. For the "human narrowness,"
the Sea is a figure of the Absolute. Faced with the Sea, men become aware of their own finitude and yearn for a higher condition. They are "leprous Kings with gold crowns," "dogs with
monkey heads, gods crossed with clay and sadness." It would be
erroneous, however, to associate Saint-John Perse with Pascal or
Lamartine. He does not see man as a "dispossessed king" or as "a
fallen god who remembers Heaven." [7] Expectation rather than
loss is the dominant feeling: man will enter the kingdom, he will
partake of divinity.

This confidence in the ultimate destiny of man is reiterated in
the second canto. The fermenting wine is a symbol of the awaited
transformation. Another symbol of metamorphosis, the bee, expresses man's accession to divinity. So does the Conqueror's entrance into the forbidden chambers of the sanctuary. Allusions to
the "laughter of Cumes" and to the "last cry of the Ephesian" may
have a similar meaning, since they could refer to the Orphic doctrine revealed to Aeneas in the underworld or to the Heraclitean
belief in the possible divinization of man. The fermenting wine,
the swarming hive, and the Conqueror's violent intrusion across
the threshold of the sanctuary thus illustrate the "triple drama"
which opens to man the Sea of the sacred: "Sea of the trance and
the transgression; Sea of the feast and the radiance; and Sea also
of action!" The entrance into the Sea is presented as a ritual which
carries man beyond the limits of his humanity. The Sea is that
locus of Being in which all forms acquire their highest mode of
existence: "the flesh itself is no longer flesh and the fire itself is no
longer flame. . . ." It embodies the very principle of life, the very
essence of being, "the god himself, consumed in his holiest species." The motif of metamorphosis recurs in its noblest form
through the reference to the transubstantiation of the Eucharist.
The Sea is also like "the forbidden Virgin in whom grows the
god": it matters little whether the verse refers to the Sibyl pos-
sessed by the god or the Christian Incarnation. In either case, the
Sea is the vehicle of the divine. The comparison of the Sea to the
sacred elephant who carries the emblems of the god during ceremonial processions is another expression of the same fundamental
meaning.

Finally, in the tireless rhythm of the tide and the violence of the storms at sea, man finds the reflection of his own restlessness. They are manifestations of the energy which drives him to pro- create or to kill, of the pride and daring which cause him to chal- lenge the unknown. The Sea is the Arena where man suddenly encounters the mystery of the sacred, the "terrible ring" where the "instant of an immortal terror" is enclosed. The poetic quest is presented as a merciless struggle where the Poet is finally cap- tured, his arms in his hands. His conquering action leads him face to face with the demonic forces which threaten to engulf him. This situation is echoed, in the third canto, by the Chorus facing the expanse of the sacred Waters. The recitation in honor of the Sea, the "immense web of poetry," is the "Sea itself, like a sacred recitative." The Reciter merely gives voice to the divine Presence which has taken possession of him and reveals itself both in the rhythm of the sea and in the rhythm of his speech. The poem and the sea are overwhelming manifestations of Being. What Saint- John Perse says of the sea also applies to poetic revelation. Since it passes all understanding, it can only be described through an ac- cumulation of contradictions: "truth in the lie and betrayal in the message; all presence and all absence, all patience and all refusal —absence, presence; order and madness—licence! . . ." The "sa- cred intrusion" is not limited to poetic creation. To be more exact, poetry is identified with every form of the human dream.

The enumeration which follows illustrates the incredible variety of this dream. It includes the beggar and the rich man, the crimi- nal and the judge, the laborer and the scholar, the defeated sol- diers and the high dignitaries, the leaders of revolutionary mobs as well as the pontiffs. For Saint-John Perse, the creative energy of the dream is the essence of man's nobility. If need be, all past loyalties must be sacrificed to the inspiring vision. The wild energy which impels man forward is as compulsive as the sexual drive. The crowd walking toward the sea in its festival dress is pursuing "the immense convulsive vulva with a thousand stream- ing crests, like the divine entrails themselves laid bare for one lightning moment." As it merges with the "universal Wife," the Sea, it will accomplish the destiny of life on earth. Its progress is depicted as the modulated answer of "all the ancient land" to the call of the Sea. The union with the Sea will bring to its conclusion the "great human phrase." [8] In its evolution, life will cross "the major threshold of the greater Orb and the signal threshold of the greatest Age," it will conquer the "forbidden world" and see the "other face of our dreams." [9]

The fourth canto is a further development of this theme. In their celebration of the Sea, men actually pay homage to the infinite plasticity of life which shall eventually gather the innumerable forms of existence in "the distant fusion of a single and same race." Such is the ultimate goal which the ritual described in *Seamarks* seeks to accomplish. It must of course be noted that the ritual does not actually take place, only its description. Furthermore, this ritual is a concrete figuration of a spiritual conquest and a symbolic expression of the poet's faith in the future of man. The procession represents the "human march" and the sea "another Immensity." For Saint-John Perse, however, there is no actual separation between the language which describes, the concrete reality which is described, and the symbolic significance of this reality. The poet of *Seamarks* does not markedly differ from the child to whom the words of a black sorcerer, "The world is like a pirogue turning around and around," brought the vision of a "world poised between shining waters" (*To Celebrate a Childhood,* 3). For Saint-John Perse, the mimicry of verbal description is no mere imitation. The language of poetry possesses the powers of a ritual formula. It brings about the manifestation of the sacred Presence: "And behold, love makes us one with the very object of these words,/And words for us they are no longer, being no longer signs or adornments,/But the thing itself which they signify and the thing itself they adorned;/Or better, reciting yourself, who are the recital, behold we become you, the recital,/And we are now you, who were to us the Irreconcilable: the very text and its substance and its sea movement,/And the very great robe of poetry with which we clothe ourselves. . . ."

In the final verses of the canto, poetic illumination is again linked to the march toward the sea and to the sexual union of humans and gods. In the concluding canto of the *Chorus,* the Poet is coming home. His only companions are the "melancholy daughters of glory," the remembrances of his ephemeral triumph. Once again, he has been deserted by his divine Visitor, but this desertion is not final: "God the stranger is in the city . . . ," and there remains, "over the deserted City, above the arena, a leaf floating in the gold of evening, still in quest of man's brow." The poet's last invocation to the Sea takes the form of a question: "Is it you,

Nomad, who this evening will pass us over to the banks of the real?" Will the return of the Sea bring at last the total revelation for which he yearns? Will it enable him to accomplish man's highest destiny, to take possession of "absolute reality," to gather in a single embrace "all the past and the future, the human and the superhuman, planetary space and total space"? [10]

V Dedication

In the *Dedication*, the question asked at the end of the *Chorus* receives a partial answer. This concluding section of *Seamarks* may be considered as an assessment of human progress. The imagery conveys a sense of triumph, of victory over darkness. The sun at its zenith seems to express the crowning achievement of the human quest. The nature of this achievement is clearly stated: "The gods awaken in the quartz." Other significant details (the Horsemen in arms at the end of Continents, the winged promontories opening their routes into the sea, the temples shining "with all their salt," the lightning bolt) also suggest that the quest has accomplished its purpose: the revelation of the sacred. Such is "the highest point of accession" to which the Poet has conducted "his whole undertaking and his people." [11] There are, in the life of individual men as well as in the history of civilizations, privileged moments when a seemingly supernatural power lifts the individual and the collectivity above their temporal limitations, when they experience eternity. In these intense moments of revelation, men seem to serve as temporary hosts for a transient god. The sacred energy of life carries them as a wave, they merge with the stream of universal Being. Such is, I believe, the meaning of the oft-quoted verse: "We who perhaps one day shall die, proclaim man as immortal at the flaming heart of the instant." The last verses of the *Dedication* simply describe the end of the ceremony. As "the man with the golden mask divests himself of his gold in honour of the Sea," he recognizes the Sea as the ultimate origin of the divinity which the ritual bestowed upon him and renounces all claims to a longer usurpation.

VI The Sea as Symbol

Critics have traced the motif of the sea in the poetry of Saint-John Perse from his earliest works to its culminating development in *Seamarks*.[12] It is equally important to bring out its symbolic value. In *Pictures for Crusoe,* the sea appears as a fecundating presence, as a source of life spreading throughout the world. In *Praises,* the springs at the bottom of the sea are another sign of generative energy. The dominant image, however, is that of the wave, which symbolizes for Saint-John Perse the eternal helix of Being, the endless rhythm of creation and destruction, of death and rebirth.[13] *Seamarks* is a conscious attempt, on the part of the poet, to develop this symbol. In the theories of Einstein which stress unity and continuity, in the myth of Shiva the Destroyer and the Fecundator, Saint-John Perse found the scientific and mythic analogues of his own vision of the cosmic process. Quantum theory, on the other hand, with its emphasis on chance and discontinuity, fosters a pessimistic view of human history. If the destiny of man is seen as the random movement of an isolated particle, if man appears as a passive fragment of matter, then the human condition has no higher meaning. Saint-John Perse cannot accept such an abdication of human pride. In *Seamarks,* he exalts the role of man in the evolution of Being, he shows man in his relation to "the great forces which create us, which make use of us, or which bind us." Man is not an isolated fragment. He is part of the "human march," he is the "insatiable migrant," driven by his need to rule the world of things, but also by his secret aspiration, in the midst of his conquering action, to that which lies beyond the temporal order, by his thirst for the divine.

In *Seamarks,* the march to the sea thus serves to illustrate the endless quest of the human spirit. Man stands "on the barest threshold, facing the splendid night of his destiny as it unfolds." The sea is "a mirror held up to his destiny," a "point of focus and radiation," a "geometrical locus," a "table of orientation," a "reservoir of eternal forces for the self-realization and self-surpassing of man." Man goes forward, spurred by his highest yearnings, individual or social, spiritual or intellectual. The march to the sea is "the exaltation of life, in the active mystery of its strength and the great unrevealed order of an eternal race." Mankind, since its darkest origins, has yearned for transcendence. The sea can therefore be considered as "our apparent frontier," as the limit of our humanity, as the mysterious presence calling to man from the future, as the lure and the means of his divinization. The word *Sea-*

marks may thus be literally interpreted as the markers which indicate the limit reached by mankind in the pursuit of its goal. In this sense, all human achievements are "seamarks," including the poem which bears this title.

CHAPTER 7

A Vision of History

THE vision of human destiny which informs the poetry of Saint-John Perse found its most complete expression in the eight cantos of *Chronicle*, a poem published in 1959, just one year before he received the Nobel Prize for Literature. In a letter addressed to Dag Hammarskjöld, Saint-John Perse characterized *Chronicle* as "a poem to the Earth, to man, and to time, all three merging . . . in the same timeless notion of Eternity." [1] *Chronicle* is a reiteration of the poet's faith in the continuity of life, in the future of the cosmos, in the permanence of time and space.

Taken in its etymological sense, the word "chronicle" refers to an account of events recorded in chronological order. This might lead some readers to stress the autobiographical content of the poem. There are, to be sure, a number of references to the poet's childhood, to his travels, to scenes which he observed, to historical events in which he took part, to his declining years, but *Chronicle* is not primarily a personal confession. Although the poem is entirely contained between quotation marks, there is no indication that the speaker must be identified with the author. In point of fact, the speaker always makes use of the plural form *we*, thus indicating that he speaks as a member of a larger collectivity, his fellow men, his contemporaries. *Chronicle* can indeed be described as an attempt to "sum up history," to assess the human adventure. [2] All through the poem, the speaker admonishes a silent audience, the "great age." On a superficial level, this expression may refer to the poet's advancing years. In another sense, a single human life reflects the evolution of the earth and the history of mankind. All three have reached a "great age," but the passage of time is not experienced as a process of attrition. The "great age" is not a prelude to death and final extinction but the culminating achievement of life in the cosmos.

I   *Great age, behold us . . .*

The "great age" addressed in the opening verse is linked to symbols of conquest and the promise of further achievements. *Pour de plus vastes cirques:* the French words suggest not only the wide expanse of circular valleys amidst the mountains but also the arenas where a higher challenge will be met. The sun setting in the west appears as a "rending of entrails, of viscera, over the whole lighted space of the Century," as the "bleeding ruptures of dream." Rather than the agony and death of an age, the imagery suggests the painful process of parturition. The identity of death and rebirth is also indicated through the juxtaposition of the "white shark belly of a cloud" and the "red stallion of the evening." The "rising stars, born of the sea," are other symbols of the heights to which the soul of man may still aspire. As in *Seamarks*, the sea appears as a "very high threshold aflame at the horizon of men." There is no breach between the continental landmass and the ocean, between past, present, and future. The use of vegetal imagery to describe the evening sky underlines the cyclical nature of time. The promise of the future takes the form of "great islands in mid-sky, robust with bushes of arbutus and juniper," which will be the site of future pasturings. In its literal sense, the French word *transhumance* refers to the seasonal moving of flocks to their mountain pastures for the summer. Another meaning is suggested by its Latin components: the migration of man beyond the boundaries of the earth and the limits of the human condition, the conquest of forbidden summits. In the final verse of the canto, this conquest is presented in terms reminiscent of the sacred marriage of the Poet and the Sea: "Fever on the heights and bed of glowing embers. Statute of brides for a night to all summits washed in gold!"

II   *Great age, you lied . . .*

The speaker's violent protest is aimed at the nihilistic prophets of despair for whom the only alternatives left to modern man are the degradation of the human anthill or the prospect of nuclear holocaust. For the speaker, the roads of men have no limit. The crack of the whip, the loud cry on the heights, the great wind which bends man over the rock—all are symbolic manifestations of the "divine turbulence" which drives man toward an elusive

God. For Saint-John Perse, God might be defined as the ultimate goal of the human march, but it is a goal which cannot be located in space and time: "our bed is not laid in place or time." Divinity resides in the "turbulence," in the dynamic process of life forever seeking to transcend itself. A man's body is only a mercenary "who will desert this evening at the bend of the road." The speaker's message reverses the legend of Persephone. Because she had eaten pomegranate seeds while she was in the lower world, Persephone could not be entirely freed from the power of Hades. The horses who pass by will soon reach the ossuary, but their mouths are still fresh from the cool sage of the meadow. Similarly, the mouths of women are still red with the "pomegranate of Cybele." All living creatures must die, but they cannot be totally subjected to the power of death once they have eaten the living fruits of the earth. In the sunset, the speaker sees the "great flame of a Century toward its crest," the portent of a still greater brilliance. The "finger of chalk beneath the untaught equation" may express the useless attempt of science to solve once and for all the mystery of man's destiny. The "great Elders" in their "rigid robes" also speak in vain. The message (religion? philosophy?) contained in their "massive books of stone" is no longer heard. The petrified wisdom of the past has lost all meaning for a new generation of men, but its failure does not lead to despair. The concluding verses offer the promise of new births: they reveal the presence of the sacred at the very heart of matter; they affirm the continuity of time.

III   *Great age, we come from all the shores of the earth . . .*

The speaker's individual experience merges with the collective destiny of the race: "Our race is ancient, our face is nameless." Through a series of evocative scenes, the personal history of the poet and the succession of his works are presented as a recapitulation of the human adventure. A symbolic thread runs through succeeding scenes: all are illustrations of the ceaseless energy of life at work in man and in nature. For the first time in the history of mankind, nuclear power threatens to bring this activity to an end: "And we were at sea perhaps, that day of eclipse and first defection, when the black she-wolf of the sky bit to the heart the ancient star of our fathers. And in the grey-green abyss with its odour of semen, colour of newborn infant's eyes, we bathed naked

—praying that for us all this good come to ill, all this ill to good."
The impending apocalypse is represented by the symbol of cosmic
death in Nordic mythology, the eclipse of the sun devoured by the
sky-wolf. Bathing naked in the sea, on the other hand, may be
interpreted as a ritual to exorcise the threat to cosmic life, as a
form of *regressus ad originem*, as a magic attempt to bring about
a new creation and to turn the destructive energy of man into the
conditions of a new birth: "So many sanctuaries laid open to the
winds, so many doctrines laid bare, like women whose thighs
were uncovered!"

The mysterious energy which drives man forward is for him a
"burning tunic"; it is also that "divine part in us that was our part
of darkness." In order to regain the love of Herakles, Dejanira
sent him a robe smeared with the poisonous blood of the Centaur
Nessus. The garment caused unbearable suffering and drove
Herakles to seek relief in death. The conquering restlessness of
man may lead to his destruction. It may also be the source of his
salvation. Here again, the sunset appears as a new dawn, as a
promise of rebirth. Generations of men succeed each other. They
know neither their origin nor their ultimate end. The fruits of the
earth are laid out before them, but there is no Host to welcome
them, no clear manifestation of a divine Presence. The God of this
world is a silent god, a god blindly seeking for self-realization. In
the final scene of the canto, the mystery of sex is used as a powerful symbol for the sacred principle which ensures the permanence
and the continuity of Being.

IV *Wandering, O Earth, we dreamed* . . .

In the first *Manifesto of Surrealism*, André Breton characterized
man as *ce rêveur définitif*.[3] The speaker of *Chronicle* would have
no quarrel with this definition. The power of the dream is for him
the prime mover of the human adventure. "Wandering, O Earth,
we dreamed . . ." is also a way of saying that dreaming *is* wandering, that the human dream takes the form of a constant metamorphosis. The true identity of man is not a fixed trust received
from his ancestors to be transmitted intact and unchanged to his
descendants. As a child, the speaker remained indifferent to the
legacy inherited from his forefathers. There was "no name" for
him in the ancestral bed bearing the family crest, in his mother's
oratory, in the golden aigrette worn by the women servants, in the

lute, the spinet or the harp, in the antique furniture, in the family heirlooms, in the tall bookcases. These objects were the material forms of his heritage. In ignoring them, he refused to allow his identity to be determined by what they represented: family traditions, religious beliefs, social position, cultural heritage. He found a more authentic self in his response to other objects which seemed to embody the raw essence of life: the smell of a giant tortoise shell, the linens of the women servants, the wax in the harness room, the flint of a black man's old flintlock, and so forth. This enumeration culminates in the evocation of "that length of chain glinting under a thunderstorm when the heavy black beast, swinging his leather pouch, rears with horns tossed high. . . ." The bull and the lightning bolt are both manifestations of the untamed cosmic energy which destroys and renews. Instinctively, the child rejected the frozen perfection of his heritage and affirmed the power of life to create new forms. The "fetid seaweed of midnight" which was the child's companion in the room under the gables where he slept may have influenced his dreams and led to his future wanderings.

V *Great age, behold us . . .*

The speaker resorts to the traditional comparison of life to a sea voyage as the evening hour brings the sailor home with his catch from the high seas. The time has come to burn the old hulks laden with seaweeds and to assess what has been accomplished: "Great age, see our takings: vain they are, and our hands free. The voyage is made and not made; the thing is said and not said." The paradoxical form of these contradictory statements suggests that the value of men's achievements does not lie in the concrete results of their actions, but in the pursuit which led to these results. The mystery of his destiny remains, but he now knows "of birth and death more than man's dream can teach." Man's conquering action brings him not only pride and honor but also "that clarity of the soul that flourishes in the great blue sword." In this verse, Saint-John Perse demonstrates once again his effective command of archetypal symbols. The sword is the concrete expression of heroic struggle, victory over darkness and death, spiritual purity and mystical aspiration. In his "wandering," the speaker has found the consequence and the confirmation of his "dreaming." From the "legends of sleep" come "all that immensity of being and profusion of being, all that passion of being and power of being," "all that great voyaging thing that the wandering Goddess raises at her heels, in the flight of her long folds, as she passes with long strides in the night. . . ." This mysterious Virgin is somewhat reminiscent of the nocturnal Visitor of *Exile*. The imagery also recalls the "rising of the great wind" in *Pictures for Crusoe* or the "gods who march in the winds" (*Winds*, I,6). The divine Creature whose presence is obscurely perceived in poetic inspiration or in the forces of nature makes it impossible to conceive of death as the annihilation of being, as the triumph of nothingness.

VI   *Like one, his hand still resting on the neck
of his mount* . . .

Faced with the approach of death, the speaker refuses to see it as an absolute limit of human life. Man is a dreamer whose fabulous vision extends far beyond the expanse of concrete reality. Here again, the sea provides a metaphoric link between the real and the dream, between past and future, between "all things equal—increate or created," the "Ocean of lands," the "Ocean of things," and the "sea beyond seas and dreams." The comparison of the evening to a Gheber is another expression of the speaker's faith in the permanence of being. The fiery sunset appears as an image of the Eternal Fire worshiped by Ghebers, of the triumph of light over darkness, of good over evil, of life over death. To the tree which "glorifies its leaf in the clarity of evening," the approaching night poses no threat. The mere existence of the tree would justify the speaker's trust in the future. Another tree will later be seen as a model for man to follow: it spreads itself "open to the night, raising to its god the ample and finely wrought burden of its giant roses." The true message of experience is to be found in the tension between the flame of life crackling on the summits and the "everlasting rain of fine ash and soft lime sifting down on the silken bed" of the abyss, in the strife between the exultation of the living soul and the awareness of the ultimate decomposition of the body. The speaker's attempt to mimic the eagle dance of the American Indian or to become one with the "jutting foreheads of white stone" emerging from the soil might be construed as an attempt to resolve this contradiction through his identification with both conflicting poles. The paradoxical conciliation of opposites suggested in the final verse accomplishes a similar purpose: "Immortal the wild sage that our hand crushes." The immortality of life balances the mortality of each living thing.

VII   *And thus, high seated . . .*

From his vantage point in space and time, the speaker gathers around him "all this great terrestrial fact." The surface of the earth is a text which reveals its geological past, but geology serves primarily as a metaphor for the history of mankind. Since time and space are symbolic equivalents, the earth is its own chronicle. On the far plains, blue shadows appear to lead "the herds of heaven so silently over the earth" (*la transhumance du ciel sur la terre*). In the first canto, the motif of *transhumance* suggested the accession of man to the divine. In canto V, the opposite takes place: the divine reveals its presence on earth. In both cantos, the motif serves the same purpose: it demonstrates that there is no impassable boundary between man and God. The speaker can state: "We are herdsmen of the future." If the "herds of heaven" can move to the pastures of the earth, so will the flocks of the earth ascend to the pastures of heaven. Those who are about to depart for *de plus hautes transhumances* may well look back and wonder: "Are we, ah, are we?—or were we ever—in all that?" And their answer is a cry of love for "the memorable face of the Earth" which can only be compared to the cry of the last Moorish king for his beloved Granada: "O memory, in man's heart, of the lost kingdom!" In the following verses, however, the glory of the sunset promises restitution: "The Sky to Westward robes itself like a Caliph . . ."; "The great rose of evening lodges a star on its breast like a golden beetle. Beyond the legends of sleep, this pledge to man under this burden of stars!" The women who "rise on the plain and march with long steps toward the red copper of existence," the "horde of Centuries" which passed this way before, all confirm the biological continuity of life and the permanence of being.

VIII   *Great age, behold us—and our mortal stride . . .*

The final canto reaffirms the speaker's faith in the destiny of the earth. In his prediction, the renewed alliance of heaven and earth, of the human and the sacred, finds a symbolic expression in the thunderstorm. Lightning is the "caduceus of the sky [descending] to mark the earth with its sign." Conversely, the aspiration of the earth for the divine takes the form of very tall trees rising toward the sky. The immortality of mankind reconciles mortal man to the "severity of the evening," to the approaching night. Death is seen as a further step in the evolution of life, as "the quivering, on the highest stem sticky with amber, of the highest leaf half-detached on its ivory claw," as a "higher adventure," as a "road traced by a new hand, and fires carried from crest to crest." It calls for a "graver song, of another steel," "pride of the soul before the soul and pride of soul growing to greatness in the great blue sword." The approaching night is not a final darkness. A new dawn will follow.

The ultimate victory of life is expressed through a revealing cluster of archetypal symbols. It includes elevation, fire, mountain tops, the sword, sovereignty, aristocratic pride, spiritual greatness, and heroic conquest, thus bringing together most of the elements used by the human imagination to exorcise the fear of darkness and death.[4] Other symbolic weapons used by the speaker in his confrontation with the mystery of death are equally significant. His offering to the night recalls the tree which opened to the night, raising to its god its splendid burden of giant roses. The speaker's gesture thus becomes a propitiatory gift to an unknown god. The tree offered its roses. The speaker offers his most precious possession, "this darkened heart of a man where hunger was, and ardour, and so much love unrevealed. . . ." The motif of metamorphosis introduced by the comparison of the heart to a "hatching of nascent wings" also tends to present death as a transitory stage in a process of becoming, as a passage toward a new form of being. A final image expresses the triumph of the human soul over the threat of time. Deserted courtyards, holy ruins and crumbling termite hills are a striking representation of a human body ravaged by time, but "the great sovereign footfalls of the soul without a lair" can still be heard in these desolate surroundings, like a "wild beast prowling a pavement of bronze." In its splendid animality, the wild beast also appears as the defiant assertion of life among the remnants of a dead civilization. The "measure of man's heart" will prove equal to the demands of the age.

IX   *A Challenge to Despair*

Chronicle thus reads as an appeal addressed not only to modern Europe, but to all mankind, to consider the fateful era in which we live, this "turning point in the course of history," as the genesis of a new future.[5] It is the poet's challenge to the nihilistic prophets of apocalyptic doom. It is also his answer to those who, like Claudel, would think that "God is a word which Saint-John Perse avoids, so to speak, religiously." As early as 1950, in his answer to Claudel, Saint-John Perse had already spoken of "the search in all things for the 'divine' which was the secret tension of [his] entire pagan life, and this intolerance, in all things, of the human limit ceaselessly growing in [him] like a cancer. . . ." *Chronicle* does not express a belief but a yearning.[6]

CHAPTER 8

The Mission of Poetry

IT must be plain, at this point, that the poetics of Saint-John Perse are deeply rooted in his most fundamental experience. For the child of *Praises*, beauty is revealed in those aspects of nature which appear as manifestations of a hidden energy, of a cosmic force: the brilliance of the sun, the rising of the stars, the violence of earthquakes and thunderstorms, the luxuriating splendor of animal and plant life. On the human plane, beauty is indissolubly linked with the presence of "the great forces which create us, which make use of us, or which bind us" (*Honneur,* p. 665). Conversely, ugliness is the visible sign of their absence. In their degradation, the City flowing like an abscess through the river to the sea, or the Library with its crumbling books, "deposits of the depths over their faeces," evoke only disgust and contempt. For Saint-John Perse, esthetic and ethical values are related through their common ontological foundation. True goodness and beauty are free from all religious, moral, and artistic conventions: they are intrinsic attributes of Being.

In his celebrated essay on Richard Wagner, Baudelaire observed that the great artist, the great poet, create first. Then, and only then, do they begin to look for the obscure laws of the creative process. In 1942, nearly forty years after the writing of *Pictures for Crusoe,* Saint-John Perse still remained unwilling to discuss the principles of his art: "On the subject of literary doctrine I have nothing at all to state. I have never relished scientific cooking." This declaration must be interpreted in its most literal sense: it did not mean that Saint-John Perse had no literary doctrine, only that he had no statement to make on this subject, at least at that time. In point of fact, this same text, the celebrated letter of 1942 to Archibald MacLeish, contained the essence of the views which he later developed in a number of articles, speeches, and letters. The theory of poetry which emerges from this body of writing is no less remarkable for its comprehensiveness than for its unity and consistence.

I *The Essence of Poetry*

In its essence, poetry is the science of Being: "Every poetic is in truth an ontology" (*Dante*). More than any other form of knowledge, it pursues absolute reality. In his Stockholm address, Saint-John Perse drew a parallel between poetry and science, pointing out that when Einstein asserted that "imagination is the real soil of all fruitful scientific ideas," this father of modern science implicitly recognized that the frontiers of poetry may well extend beyond the vistas opened by the scientist. In the person of Léon-Paul Fargue, Saint-John Perse has paid homage to a poet whose intuition goes further than even the boldest speculations of science.[1] In its exploration of the human mystery, poetry can also claim greater powers than philosophy. Dante was well trained in Thomist scholasticism, but in the *Divine Comedy* "the threshold of metaphysics is crossed . . . only by poetic knowledge" (*Dante*). Saint-John Perse also refers to Heidegger's interest in the poetry of Hölderlin or Trakl (*Honneur,* p. 622). This fact confirms his belief that "when the philosophers abandon the metaphysical threshold, it falls to the poet to take upon himself the role of metaphysician . . ." (*Poetry*). Religion itself yields to poetry, even in that most religious of poets, Dante. In an age when religion has lost all meaning for so many, poetry alone maintains alive the sense of the sacred. To a civilization obsessed by material values, poetry appears as the last refuge of divinity.

More than a way of knowledge, poetry is a "way of life, of life in its totality." To the men of his age, the poet offers the "vision of a new humanism: of authentic universality, of psychic integrity": "In one embrace, as in one great living strophe, [poetry] gathers to its present all the past and the future, the human and the superhuman, planetary space and total space" (*Poetry*). This definition must be taken literally. Poetic vision illuminates Being in all of its dimensions: past and future, physical and spiritual, human and divine, temporal and eternal, real and imaginary.[2] This is why Saint-John Perse feels authorized to claim such powers for the poet: "by his absolute adhesion to what exists, the poet keeps us in touch with the permanence and unity of Being. And his message is one of optimism. To him, one law of harmony gov-

erns the whole world of things. Nothing can occur there which by
its nature its incommensurable with man. The worst catastrophes
of history are but seasonal rhythms in a vaster cycle of repetitions
and renewals. The Furies who cross the stage, torches high, do
but throw light upon one moment in the immense plot as it unfolds itself through time. Growing civilizations do not perish from
the pangs of one autumn; they merely shed their leaves"
(*Poetry*). This conception of cosmic order and of human history
is clearly patterned on the order of nature, on the cycle of seasons,
on the death and rebirth of vegetation. Destruction is merely the
prelude to a new creation.

Six centuries before Christ, Heraclitus had stated that "all
things come to pass through the compulsion of strife," but he also
recognized that "strife is justice," that change remains within the
bounds of a cosmic order: "The sun will not overstep its measures." The similarity of their views has been recognized by Saint-
John Perse himself (*Honneur*, p. 655). In the Indian myth of
Shiva, the god of destruction and regeneration, he found a similar
basis for optimism (*Poetry*). In Saint-John Perse's vision of history, the opposing forces of destruction and renewal obey a law of
harmony in which all opposites balance each other, although the
individuality of opposing elements is maintained. In the human
drama, suffering and death have no less reality than joy and rebirth. This contrasting structure conforms to the pattern of ancient drama. Man appears as the protagonist of a Greek tragedy
in his struggle with an all-powerful fate.

This dramatic structure exerts such a fascination over the poet's
imagination that he instinctively fits contemporary events into its
pattern. The text which he wrote as a tribute to the widow of
President Kennedy offers a remarkable example. She is seen as the
chosen victim pursued by the Furies of ancient drama, as a tragic
figure elected to exemplify the nobility of human heroism in the
face of suffering and death.[3] History thus becomes a ritual *agon*:
the fear and anguish of mortal Fate are exorcised through the
symbolic struggle of the hero, who in his defeat bears witness for
the greatness of man. In Saint-John Perse's vision of the historical
process, this dramatic structure is endlessly repeated. This does
not mean that the history of Being may be reduced to a series of
identical cycles. The traditional structure of the Eternal Return is
combined, for Saint-John Perse, with a teleological vision of his-

tory. The evolution of life on earth is seen as a march toward a higher destiny, although the ultimate goal of this *anabasis* remains shrouded in mystery.

II   *The Mission of Poetry*

In a letter addressed to the editor of *The Berkeley Review*, Saint-John Perse draws a sharp contrast between English poetry and French poetry, but the words English and French are used primarily as convenient tags to distinguish between two types of poetry. The first one is "born of meditation, not of a trance," it follows "the line of a modulation, not the real complexity of an incantation." Its rational discourse deals clearly and logically with explicit ideas or themes. Its chief purpose is to confirm a traditional vision of Being. Another poetry (and Saint-John Perse is obviously speaking of his own) seeks the integration of its living self with its living object, the total identification of subject and object, of poet and poem. Instead of signalling or representing, "it becomes the very thing which it 'apprehends,' which it evokes or calls forth." It does not imitate, it "*is* the thing itself, in its movement and its duration" (*Honneur,* pp. 656–57). This poetry can indeed claim to show "the strongest passion for and the keenest appreciation of 'absolute reality,' to that extreme limit of complicity where reality seems to shape itself within the poem" (*Poetry*). Poetry is therefore the human activity which best enables man to merge with the creative energy of life, to be carried by the "helix of being," to be borne by the wave which since Troy (the mythic origin of human history in Western culture) "still rolls its haunch toward us." [4]

The privileged position which Saint-John Perse claims for the poet is entirely justified since he, more than anyone else, is "concerned with man in the plenitude of his being" (*Poetry*). Conversely, poetry exacts such a full understanding of its essence and such a commitment to its mission that many so-called poets do not truly deserve this noblest of titles. Poetry, as it is defined by Saint-John Perse, has "no place for anything Pythian" (*Poetry*). Authentic poets do not surrender to the dark forces of the unconscious, especially with the help of hallucinogenic drugs. On the other hand, poetic vision cannot be subjected to the mutilating effects of logic (*Winds,* II, 5,6). Dante, to whom Saint-John Perse pays the highest homage, invoked the assistance of the Delphic divinity, "ravisher of the soul and the spirit beyond the province of intellect" (*Dante*). Apollo, the god of poetry, is of course the god of mantic possession as well as the god of light. For Saint-John Perse, there is "no pure poetry . . . without complete reliance upon the subconscious. But the subconscious must be treated rigorously, must be mastered, by reason." [5] He may, on occasion, slight the role of reason in poetic creation. Thus Fargue is praised for having always been "intelligent enough to leave intelligence at the door of the poem." [6] On the other hand, Saint-John Perse shows the poet "mindful of his lucidity, jealous of his authority, and holding clear in the wind the high noon of his vision." His mission is defined as the "clarifying of messages" (*Winds*, III, 6). The poet illuminates "the dark of the human soul herself and the dark of the mystery which envelops human existence" (*Poetry*). The authentic universality and the psychic integrity which the poet seeks to promote must include the irrational forces of the unconscious and the unknown forces of life which surround us, but not at the expense of other human faculties.

There is no question, however, that Saint-John Perse places the value of inspiration far above that of calculation: "I am interested only in the living creation, which comes unsolicited in the night. From time to time, I complete a poem, I polish, I prune, etc., but that is not what interests me . . . I am the opposite of Valéry, who constantly revised what he wrote. He was a great mind, an artist, but not a *poet*." [7] Having thus rejected the Surrealists' complete subservience to the unconscious and Valéry's excessive dependence on the intellect, Saint-John Perse proceeds to other exclusions. True poetry has no place for the "art of the embalmer nor of the decorator," for "cultured pearls," "fakes or emblems." It will not replace the blood and mire of living reality with the dead perfection of Byzantium. It has no use for the refined artificiality of a des Esseintes. Authentic poets refuse to divorce art from life, to seek refuge in an ivory tower or in the private world of their dreams. They are no hunger artists who yearn, as did Mallarmé, for the purity of nothingness, nor are they propagandists at the service of an ideology. They will not proclaim, with Verlaine, *de la musique avant toute chose:* poetry must not be content to be a "mere feast of music."

What then, is the poet's mission? Saint-John Perse ends his Stockholm address with this message: "And it is enough for the poet to be the guilty conscience of his time." The poet breaks the "bonds of habit," he frees his fellow men from the prison of a materialistic culture, he illuminates the future: "It is for the poet, in his wholeness, to bear witness to the twofold vocation of man: to hold up before the spirit a mirror sensitive to his spiritual possibilities; to evoke, in our own century, a vision of the human condition more worthy of man as he was created; to connect ever more closely the collective soul to the currents of spiritual energy in the world" (*Poetry*). Saint-John Perse's theory of poetic creation must be considered in the light of these pronouncements.

III   *The Poetic Process*

The ceaseless flow of Being forever creates forms which are then destroyed and replaced with new forms. All living creatures are born, live, and die to be succeeded by new individuals. Entire species appear on earth, flourish for ages, and eventually disappear. So do comets, planets, and stars. Civilizations which at one time occupied the center stage of history have vanished without a trace. Poetry is the mirror in which the movement of Being is revealed. Poetic creation not only reproduces the creative rhythm of Being, it is an actual manifestation of its energy. Poetry is "movement in its inception as well as in its growth and in its final expression" (*Honneur*, p. 655). This is why poetry makes it possible for man "to live better and farther." [8] It links man to the unifying principle of Being: "By means of analogical and symbolic thinking, by means of the far-reaching light of the mediating image and its play of correspondences, by way of a thousand chains of reactions and unusual associations, by virtue also of a language through which is transmitted the supreme rhythm of Being, the poet clothes himself in a transcendental reality to which the scientist cannot aspire" (*Poetry*).

This process appears in its simplest form in the early works of Saint-John Perse, where it may be identified as symbolic perception rather than symbolic thinking. Water is perceived as "green sunlight," just as the City is "yellow with rancour" and the sea "rosy with lust." This spontaneous symbolization of experience may be considered as the most elementary form of the poetic process. It is also the original source of myth and ritual. The mind to which water appears as "green sun" also creates its own gods. In her study of symbolic transformation, Susanne K. Langer observes

that "this activity belongs to about the earliest period of childhood, that memory can recover. . . . From this dawn of memory
. . . to adolescence, there is a constant decrease in such dreamlike experience. . . ." [9] In the artist, the power of symbolic transformation is not lost. It is developed and refined to such a degree
that it claims as its own the privilege of perceiving the essential
pattern of the universe. Poetic inspiration takes place when this
pattern is revealed in an overwhelming illumination. In the innumerable forms of Being, the poet actually sees the effect of a
single principle, of a wave of energy flowing through space and
time, destroying and renewing all appearances.

In a penetrating study, the French poet and critic Claude Vigée
has demonstrated that the entire work of Saint-John Perse may be
characterized as the apprehension of this energy in its successive
manifestations (*Honneur,* pp. 345–52). The ecstatic submission or
the naïve rapture of the early poems is replaced, in the poems of
exile, by the unequal struggle with the Angel of the Thunderstorm, with the demonic power which takes possession of the human soul. The brutal rape by a merciless god is succeeded, in
Seamarks, by the nuptial alliance. Each poem merely records the
manifestation, within the individual consciousness, of Being itself.
Being (and this entity includes not only what is, but also what has
been, what shall be, and what may be, the world of dream as well
as the concrete world of things) is experienced as "one long
phrase without pause forever unintelligible" (*Exile*), as "a Bible
of shadows and freshness" (*Winds*), as "the greater narration of
things throughout the world" (*Seamarks*), as "one great living
strophe" (*Poetry*). The world in its totality is perceived as a text,
as a message which the poet simply transcribes. This vision of the
poetic process is reflected in Saint-John Perse's themes and motifs;
in his use of words, rhythms, and sounds; and in his criticism.

IV *Themes and Motifs*

In his impressive study of Saint-John Perse's imagery, Jean-
Pierre Richard explores the symbolic value of contrasting themes
and motifs.[10] In *Praises,* voluptuous repose in the intimacy of nature is opposed to the call of the sea. The horsemen of *Anabasis*
must fight the temptations of urban comfort and stability in order
to resume their conquering expedition. In *Winds,* the accumulated dust or silt left by a dead past must be scattered by the

winds or flushed out by new waters. In the poet's preference for the aridity of the desert, the empty expanse of a beach, the hardness of bones and stones, the clean edge of a blade, the biting taste of salt, the sudden flash of lightning, J.-P. Richard recognizes images of spiritual aspiration or conquest. The sheltered comfort of country orchards or the cozy confines of a quiet provincial town, on the other hand, are symbols of weakness, of softness. They represent the "stable of happiness" in which the conquering spirit of man is imprisoned. The elementary forces of nature, wind, rain, thunder, and lightning, embody the cosmic energy which restores the world to its primeval fertility, just as wars and revolutions are manifestations of the spiritual energy which frees man from the paralyzing grip of a dying order.

Richard finds in the motif of the threshold the symbolic expression of the poet's division between the attraction of order and stability and the urge to go beyond all limits. I would also interpret this motif as an expression of the poet's conflict between his loyalty to the human and his aspiration to the nonhuman and relate it to another recurring theme, the intermittent manifestation of a divine Presence. In the rolling thunder, Crusoe heard the great blasts of his Lord's voice, and the tropical breeze, for the child of *Praises*, was the breathing of a god. The poet of *Exile* faces once more the faithless goddess who deserted his bed. He is, in *Winds*, the victim of the god's brutal assault, but in *Seamarks* the ritual union of a human creature and a divine being announces the eventual divinization of man. Symbols of metamorphosis illustrate the same theme. The pupa which changes into a winged bee seems to offer a model for the future transformation of man, for the "human clay where the expected face of the god is taking shape" (*Seamarks*). The theme of mimicry is still more significant. The mirror and the mask, the drama and the dance are symbolic representations of poetic creation and express its ritual function. The ritual act does not merely mime a sacred reality: it recreates its presence. The various events described in the poems of Saint-John Perse, the foaling of a colt, the growth of a tree, the endless surge of a wave, the ceaseless flow of rivers, the swarming of bees, the road where glowing embers never turn to ashes, are more than symbolic representations of the energy at work in the cosmos, of the life force which actuates the "human march," man's eternal ascent toward the summits of the future. They do

not imitate what is, they give shape to what shall be, they antici-
pate the ultimate unity which will fuse the totality of Being into a
single harmony.

The poetry of Saint-John Perse may be interpreted as the symbolic achievement of this goal. The various artifacts which he remembers from courtesy visits to European museums illustrate the
disconnected and fragmentary appearance assumed by the creative energy of Being (*Honneur*, p. 653). The reality presented in
the poems of Saint-John Perse appears equally fragmented. The
wealth and the precision of his vocabulary betray the poet's effort
to stress the distinctive and separate character of each particular
element in his universe. His use of all fields of knowledge reflects
a similar purpose. The most recondite or technical items of information serve to emphasize the infinite variety and heterogeneity
of Being. There is, at first sight, no visible link between the Aztec
crystal skull from Pre-Columbian times and a collection of fantas-
tic engravings for the lining of cigar boxes. Nor does it always
seem possible to discover a common element in the lengthy
enumerations which are such a prominent feature in the poems of
Saint-John Perse. Can there be a significant relationship between
the public display, after the wedding night, of bedsheets stained
by the ruptured hymen of the bride, the building of terraces for
meat-drying, the playing of dice, and the eating of fritters (*Anabasis*, X)? And yet, from the listing of such seemingly incongruous
modes of human behavior, there emerges a sense of order and
unity. There is no fundamental difference between the man who
plots the course of a hurricane or the poet seized by inspiration,
between Dido and Malinche, between the Spanish Conquistadores and the uranium prospectors, between the men who painted
in the caves of Altamira or Lascaux and the accordion players in
the stokeholds of modern ships.[11] Below the chaos of superficial
appearances, these enumerations reveal the deep identity of the
"forces which create us, which make use of us or which bind us"
(*Honneur*, p. 655).

The poet's vision perceives the secret analogies which the poem
makes visible through its imagery. Poetry reveals, for instance,
that the world of man and the world of nature are one. Through
the imagery which assimilates wars and revolutions to the destructive action of the wind, the poet creates a vision of history which
suggests that the adventure of man in the universe is more than a

tale told by an idiot. In the culture of our times, the poem fulfills
the function of myth in more primitive societies. It presents modern man with a symbolic structure which enables him to overcome
the contradictions of his experience; it restores a sense of order
and unity to a fragmented and absurd reality.

V *The Language of Poetry*

In his Stockholm address, Saint-John Perse characterized the
language of poetry as "a language through which is transmitted
the supreme rhythm of Being." The poet's use of meter seeks to
render the movement and the duration of the object depicted in
the poem, to follow with the utmost fidelity its measure and
rhythm, "broadly and at length when, for instance, the sea or the
wind are concerned; tightly and promptly in dealing with the
lightning flash." [12] Saint-John Perse is obviously not suggesting
that poetry ought to compete with program music. He merely rejects the notion that it must submit to the rigid pattern of conventional French prosody. What Saint-John Perse has to say about
Fargue's contribution to the prose poem applies equally to his
own. Fargue's poetic mode, "without visible meter or rhythmic
monotony," manages to retain the rhythm and the melody which
constitute the essential harmony of traditional verse. [13]

In the poetry of Saint-John Perse, the rhythm and the melody
are provided through various devices: symmetrical clauses, identical or echoing phrases, recurring cadences, alliterations, as-
sonances, internal rhymes, substitutions of vowels and consonants,
alternation of syllables. A few examples, which must perforce be
given in French, will suffice to illustrate the elaborate complexity
of a verbal texture in which sense and sound are inextricably connected: "Végétales *ferveurs* [6 syllables], ô clartés ô *faveurs!* . . .
[6 syllables]" (*Praises*); "Ah! *toute chose* *v*aine au *v*an de la
mémoire [12 syllables], *ah! toute chose* insane aux fifres de l'exil
[12 syllables]: *le pur* n*autile des eaux* libres [8 syllables], *le pur*
mo*bile* d*e* n*os* songes [8 syllables]" (*Exile*); "Transfuges *sans*
mess*age* [6 syllables], ô Mimes *sans* vis*age* [6 syllables]" (*Rains*);
"*Le vin nouveau n'est pas plus* v*rai* [8 syllables], *le lin nouveau*
n'est pas plus frais [8 syllables]" (*Winds*). It must be repeated
that Saint-John Perse has no wish to make of poetry a "mere feast
of music." Echoing rhythms and sounds primarily serve to reflect
the complex network of secret analogies and associations present

in the whole world of things. The harmony of the poem expresses the law of harmony which, in the poet's vision, governs the entire cosmos. A similar effect is created through the conscious exploitation of ambiguity.

In the French language, according to Saint-John Perse, words have reached such a level of abstraction that they no longer bear a visible relation to concrete reality, as would be the case in languages which make use of ideographic writing. In French, words have come to be used as fiduciary money, as a convenient means of exchange. They only have the fictive value which they derive from the use to which they are put. In the course of a prolonged evolution, all traces of the original referent have vanished. Saint-John Perse sees this deprivation as a gain. In breaking away from the original referent, words have acquired ambiguity and multivalence. They have, so to speak, become disembodied, free to assume other functions than pure denotation. This state of affairs enables the poet to exploit the possibilities opened, for instance, by forgotten etymologies. To take a simple example, the current meaning of *aubaine* (godsend, windfall) is no longer related to its etymon *aubain* (alien). Neither word is etymologically related to the word *aube*, which has the dual meaning of dawn and alb. This makes it possible for the poet to "play a mysterious and allusive game of secret analogies and correspondences, and even of multiple associations, at the limit of understanding. Sometimes, along several parallel or divergent lines, several meanings are suggested simultaneously." [14] The "complicity of meaning" suggested by the echoing sounds emphasizes the sense of harmony which the poet seeks to create.[15]

A comparable effect can be produced by the symmetry of the design. The opening verse of *Rains* ("The banyan of the rain takes hold of the City") is echoed, near the end of the poem, by the verse: "The banyan of the rain loses its hold on the City." The dead tree presented in the first canto of *Winds* is succeeded, in the final section, by the new tree which will take its place. The ordered architecture of the poem reflects the order which underlies the heterogeneity of reality. It would be misleading, however, to suggest that the poetry of Saint-John Perse submits to the rational order of logic. In his opinion, "poetic usurpation operates far beyond the space controlled by reason." [16] Saint-John Perse has repeatedly stressed the importance of ellipsis in his works. The poet's vision leaps across the expanse of Being, omitting each and every step required by the intellect to establish a connecting bridge. This is why Saint-John Perse feels justified in defending modern poetry in general, and his own poems in particular, against the accusation of verbal facility and rhetorical amplification: their most prolonged verbal sequences actually represent a "sum of contractions, omissions and ellipses" (*Honneur,* p. 656). *Anabasis* was reduced from two hundred to sixty pages, *Winds* from six hundred to two hundred, *Seamarks* from seven hundred to two hundred.[17] The works of Saint-John Perse are the product of a refining process which leaves only their poetic essence. For Saint-John Perse, the language of poetry is language at its highest intensity.

VI *Values in Literature*

Although Saint-John Perse has steadfastly refused to consider himself as a professional man of letters and to lead the so-called literary life, he has, over the years, paid homage to literary figures whose friendship he valued and whose works he admired. From his "Letter on Jacques Rivière," published in 1925, to his most recent tribute to the French poet René Char, he has constantly singled out for praise, in the man or his writings, those qualities which most closely reflect his own vision of human destiny. These virtues, as it clearly appears from his speech in commemoration of Aristide Briand or from the text written after President Kennedy's assassination, are not the exclusive privilege of the man of letters. Statesmen as well as poets, scientists no less than artists may share in the same pursuit: the total fulfilment of man. Einstein was the architect of the greatest intellectual synthesis in the area of science. Briand embodied the hopes of his age for political harmony and universal peace. President Kennedy fought not only for the welfare of his own countrymen but also for the rights and freedoms of all men. In other times, Dante unified the language of his people and thus forged the instrument of their political and cultural unity. If Briand deserved to be called the Apostle of the Federal Union of Europe, Valery Larbaud had an equal claim to the title of *Larbaud l'Européen*. In his person, the literatures of Europe and America transcended the narrow limits of national boundaries and merged into a common patrimony for the enjoyment of all. The founders and directors of the review *Cahiers du*

Sud extended their allegiance beyond the limits of the Mediterranean tradition as they rediscovered the legacy of the Celtic culture. Each in his own way, Gide and Tagore, Rivière and Fargue
demonstrated the same receptivity to all aspects of human experience, the same curiosity for every new modulation of the human
soul. All of these men made a significant contribution to the formation of a new humanism, to the formation of a broader vision
of man. In their person, their action or their creation, all illustrated human nobility; all exemplified man's capacity for greatness; all served higher ends than physical comfort, material gain,
or petty ambition. Esthetic values, for Saint-John Perse, are no
more than the manifestation, on the artistic or the literary plane,
of the spiritual energy which inspires mankind in its relentless
quest for transcendence.

True art springs from the very heart of Being. It plunges its
roots to the depths of the human clay. Art owes its life to the
concrete reality from which it springs. Gide and Claudel, Larbaud
and Fargue, Adrienne Monnier and Jacques Rivière, all take their
place in the living continuity of the French tradition. In Dante,
Tagore, and Ungaretti, Saint-John Perse honors the poet's fidelity
to his sources. Paradoxically, the artist's fidelity to his origins is
also the foundation of his universality, since the eternal energy of
Being reveals its presence, not in abstract generality, but in the
concrete particularity of a landscape, a language, a culture, a people. This does not mean that great art should be identified with
local color: Saint-John Perse has often declared his disdain of
exoticism. The art which can extend the boundaries of human experience to their furthest limit is the art which expresses reality in
all its living vitality. True universality is achieved through the integration of all forms of human experience within the collective
soul of mankind.

Human experience must not, however, be limited to the "empire of the real." Great artists do more than affirm the "terrestrial
vocation" (*Dante*). Tagore proudly affirms the "primogeniture of
the dream." [18] In the poets Fargue and Schéhadé, there lives an
"alien guest" whose voice speaks through the poem. Dante conducted his quest to "the margin of the great free spaces where
the divine unfolds." He was a poet, "this born rebel who lays
claim in man to more than man." He sought the "secret ways of

the ineffable and the inconceivable" and "reached that blinding point of rupture of which there is no memory" (*Dante*). Claudel, on the other hand, was "the least mystical of believers." He suspected poetic illumination and trusted only reason and logic in his quest for God.[19] In Jacques Rivière, Saint-John Perse also seems to deplore the suppression of imagination, the mistrust of instinct. When he observes that Gide avidly courted "all the risks of rupture, without rupture," he clearly regrets that Gide should have yielded to the gravitational pull of "the earthly and the human." [20] In renouncing all forms of poetic vision, Gide repudiated the mystery of transcendence.

In the age-old quarrel between intellect and intuition, between logic and imagination, Saint-John Perse refuses to choose one side to the exclusion of the other. In the history of French literature, the mistrust of divinatory intuition deprived poetry of its essential instrument: poets were "riders without horses." [21] Saint-John Perse clearly favors the "human suppleness and the free movement" of Renaissance humanism over the "rationalist aridity of the 18th century and the great inflexible order of the 17th." [22] He indicts French Romanticism for its failure to legitimize the rights of the unconscious and blames Hugo for this failure. For the sake of public fame and material success, Hugo sacrificed the mystery of poetry. The revolution which should have been accomplished by the French Romantics was the work of later poets: Nerval and Baudelaire, Lautréamont and Rimbaud, Corbière and the Symbolists. On the other hand, Saint-John Perse welcomes the participation of the intellect in poetic creation. True artists assign a subordinate role to the intellect: they do not exclude it. The patient elaboration required for the successful completion of a poem is "the filial obligation of the poet to his language as creator" (*Dante*). The devotion to form should not be confused with the artificial ornamentation of preciosity. Gide's and Larbaud's respect for stylistic perfection was a manifestation of artistic integrity, of literary honor. The artist's patient labor pursues its own invisibility. In a literary work, the inseparability of form and content is the hallmark of esthetic authenticity.

Saint-John Perse's considerations on values in literature clearly exceed the bounds of literature as such. *Birds,* a poetic meditation which he composed as a companion text for Braque's series of plates *L'Ordre des Oiseaux,* extends these considerations to the realm of painting. *Birds* is a meditation on esthetics as well as on poetics.

VII   *A Meditation on Art: Birds*

The central theme is indicated by the epigraph, which is taken from the Latin poet Persius: "more than a kite can soar over." Even the widest expanse cannot satisfy the yearning of the spirit for the infinite. In their constant search for an endless summer, migratory birds exemplify the energy of life in its eternal quest for an elusive goal. They are of the earth, and not of the earth. Through their dual allegiance to land and air, birds also express the division of life between matter and spirit and its perpetual pursuit of transcendence. In the slim patch of color which he deposits on his canvas, the painter captures a "true sum," "the thing itself as inevitably given," "a pure fragment of space" which retains its ties with the totality of Being (*Birds,* 3). Braque's birds resemble the magnetic needle of the compass: they make visible an invisible force, the impetus which enables life in its conquering flight to break the thread of gravity which keeps it earthbound. On the artist's canvas, the birds play the same role as words on the poet's page: "they are carried, like words, by the universal rhythm" and the message which they spell endows man with a new audacity: "Go beyond! . . ." (*Birds,* 8, 9). Their flight spans the totality of the universe and takes them to the frontiers of Being.

The birds painted by Braque represent no particular species, order, or genus, nor do they owe anything to myth, legend, or literature. They express one thing only: the archetypal constant of the bird in the poetic space of man. This constant has nothing to do with abstract knowledge. It springs from the primordial impression made by a bird in flight on the imagination of man. In *Birds,* as in *Seamarks,* in the poem as well as in the painting, art is the faithful transcription of reality as it spontaneously reveals itself to the imagination of the artist. Although Saint-John Perse advances no explanation for this theory of artistic creation, it may be related to a theoretical foundation. The concrete reality of the bird activates the primitive human response to elevation and verticality, to the sky as the source of all light, to the dynamic thrust of the arrow or the spear. In the artist, this response is characterized by its range and its intensity. His creation has the power to affect the fundamental structures which shape our experience. Poem and painting bring back to life the universal archetypes which, since time began, have haunted the human imagination.

VIII *Conclusion*

The universal appeal of Saint-John Perse's poetry is indicated by a simple observation: his poems are read all over the world. Translations have appeared in most European countries, in North and South America, in Japan and in India. French, American, Spanish, and Japanese reviews have paid him the homage of devoting entire issues to his writings. If such geographical considerations do not constitute the best evidence of authentic universality, a better criterion might be found in the attention which the poetry of Saint-John Perse has attracted from the most opposite quarters. His admirers include Henry Miller, T. S. Eliot, André Breton, Paul Claudel, Roger Nimier, and Roger Garaudy. Staunch Catholics, leading Surrealists, aristocratic conservatives, true believers of the Marxist persuasion and prophets of *négritude* have proved equally enthusiastic in their acclaim.

Can this general appeal be explained by Saint-John Perse's symbolism, which reflects the fundamental structures of the human imagination as they exist in all men? Chances are that readers rather sense the poet's genuine admiration for all manifestations of human greatness. They respond to the fact that he does not equate the human achievement of a given civilization with its gross national product. At a stage of history when mankind has reached an unprecedented degree of division, the poetry of Saint-John Perse reintroduces the vision of a new community. To a world faced with the possibility of nuclear extinction, it affirms the perenniality of life. Unlike the theories of progress through reason and science which the nineteenth century inherited from the Age of Enlightenment, his faith in the future of man cannot be reduced to some naïve form of meliorism. In the poetry of Saint-John Perse, readers do not see a theory of history which may appear rationally persuasive. They respond to a vision which answers the deepest human needs. "Authentic universality" and "psychic integrity" are indeed the obvious cures for the most common ailments of our times: social alienation and psychic fragmentation.

Notes and References

Preface

1. It is quite possible that Saint-John Perse selected his pseudonym simply because the word "saint-léger," in the First *Supplément* to the *Grand Larousse du XIXe siècle*, is immediately preceded by the name of a nineteenth-century British writer: SAINT-JOHN (Percy). The name "Saint-John Perse" would then result from the transformation of "Percy" into "Perse." If such is the case, the choice of this pseudonym was largely dictated by chance, and it would have nothing to do with Saint-John de Crèvecoeur, Saint John the Baptist, the Caribbean island of Saint-John, the Latin poet Persius, or ancient Persia.

2. The single exceptions are *Anabasis,* which was translated by T. S. Eliot and published in London (Faber and Faber, 1930), and *Chanté par Celle qui fut là . . . ,* which has recently been translated by Richard Howard and published by the Princeton University Press (1970). A revised edition of *Anabasis* has been published in America by Harcourt, Brace and Co. (New York, 1949).

Chapter One

1. "Arise ye soon, ye desired storms, which shall carry away René to the expanse of another life . . ." (Chateaubriand, *René*); "And I am like the withered leaf;/Carry me away, O stormy Northern winds" (Lamartine, "L'Isolement"); (Shelley, "Ode to the West Wind").

2. In *Honneur à Saint-John Perse*, pp. 345–46.

3. See M. Eliade, *Traité d'histoire des religions*, pp. 360–63.

4. A. Knodel, *Saint-John Perse*, pp. 22, 24.

5. This combination is a recurrent symbol in the poetry of Saint-John Perse. It fuses water, fire, and the living energy of vegetation into a single entity, thus suggesting the unity and the creative power of Being.

6. For a different interpretation, see A. Knodel, *Saint-John Perse*, p. 24.

7. See M. Parent, *Saint-John Perse et quelques devanciers*, pp. 170–171.

8. G. Durand, *Les structures anthropologiques de l'imaginaire*, pp. 61–121. See also A. Knodel, *Saint-John Perse*, pp. 28–29.

Chapter Two

1. R. Poggioli, *The Spirit of the Letter*, p. 228.
2. Princesse Marie Bonaparte, *Psychanalyse et anthropologie*, p. 11.
3. M. Parent, *Saint-John Perse et quelques devanciers*, pp. 188–89.
4. See R. Little: "Language as Imagery in Saint-John Perse," *Forum for Modern Language Studies*, vol. VI, no. 2 (April 1970), pp. 123–139; M. Parent, *Saint-John Perse et quelques devanciers*, pp. 231–32; M. Eliade, *Traité d'histoire des religions*, pp. 228–80.
5. My main sources for this paragraph are: G. Durand, *Les structures anthropologiques de l'imaginaire*; M. Eliade, *Traité d'histoire des religions*; J. Campbell, *The Masks of God*.
6. M. Saillet, *Saint-John Perse, poète de gloire*, pp. 50–52.
7. Mallarmé, "Mes bouquins refermés sur le nom de Paphos"; P. Valéry, "Le Cimetière marin."
8. Malraux, *Les Noyers de l'Altenburg*, pp. 127–42.

Chapter Three

1. See B. Weinberg, *The Limits of Symbolism*, pp. 368, 374.
2. Saint-John Perse seems to have made some use of Arrian's *Anabasis* and Plutarch's *Life of Alexander*. He may also have borrowed some episodes from Ammianus Marcellinus' account of the military expeditions conducted by the Roman Emperor Julian against the Persians. Finally, Herodotus and Strabo may have provided him with information concerning the rites and customs of Asian populations. See F. Carmody, "Saint-John Perse, Several Oriental Sources," *Comparative Literature Studies*, vol. II, no. 2, pp. 125–51.
3. See R. Poggioli, *The Spirit of the Letter*, p. 223; A. Bosquet, *Saint-John Perse*, pp. 96–99; C. Roy, *Descriptions critiques*, pp. 137–138.
4. The main interpretations have been offered by Lucien Fabre (*Honneur à Saint-John Perse*, pp. 406–7); T. S. Eliot, Preface to the American translation of *Anabasis*; R. Poggioli, *The Spirit of the Letter*, pp. 230–37; A. Bosquet, *Saint-John Perse*, pp. 34–41; A. Knodel, *Saint-John Perse*, pp. 40–53; B. Weinberg, *The Limits of Symbolism*, pp. 381–415; M. Parent, *Saint-John Perse et quelques devanciers*, pp. 193–205; R. Little, "Une image de la dialectique mouvement-stasis dans *l'Anabase* de Saint-John Perse," *Revue des Sciences Humaines*, Avril–Juin 1971, pp. 229–35; K. R. Srinivasa Iyengar, "St.-John Perse's *Anabase*: A Study," *The Aryan Path*, vol. XXIII, no. 1, January 1962, pp. 15–18 and no. 2, February 1962, pp. 57–62.
5. See Edmond Rostand, *Chanteclair*, Act I, sc. ii; P. Valéry,

"Ebauche d'un Serpent," stanzas 3 and 4; Yeats, "Among School Children." If this reading has any validity, Saint-John Perse must be ranked with Plato's most violent foes. His interest in Pre-Socratic philosophers is well known (*Honneur à Saint-John Perse*, p. 655).

6. M. Parent, *Saint-John Perse et quelques devanciers*, p. 239.

7. The information concerning the offering of the quail and the flask-merchant was provided by the poet himself. See A. J. Knodel, "Towards an Understanding of *Anabase*," *Publications of the Modern Language Association*, June 1964, p. 336.

8. See G. Durand, *Les structures anthropologiques de l'imaginaire*, pp. 184–286.

9. M. Parent, *Saint-John Perse et quelques devanciers*, p. 203; R. Little, "Une image de la dialectique mouvement-stasis dans l'*Anabase* de Saint-John Perse," *Revue des Sciences Humaines*, Avril–Juin 1971, pp. 232–33.

10. The preceding quotations may be found in *Honneur à Saint-John Perse*, pp. 621–22, 653.

11. A. Bosquet, *Saint-John Perse*, p. 33.

12. *Honneur à Saint-John Perse*, pp. 665–67. Saint-John Perse disclaims any influence from Teilhard de Chardin, although he recognizes a certain affinity with the thought of the Jesuit philosopher (See K. Raine, "Saint-John Perse, Poet of the Marvellous," *Encounter*, October 1967, pp. 51–61).

Chapter Four

1. In *Honneur à Saint-John Perse*, 105.

2. M. Parent, "Le thème de l'orage dans *Exil* de Saint-John Perse," *Boletim de filologia*, XIX (1960), p. 212. For other interpretations, see A. Knodel, *Saint-John Perse*, p. 63; J. Roger Little, "Elements of the Jason-Medea myth in *Exil* by Saint-John Perse," *The Modern Language Review*, LXI (1966), pp. 422–25.

3. M. Parent, *Saint-John Perse et quelques devanciers*, p. 223.

4. The factual information used in this study of the *Poem to a Foreign Lady* is to be found in A. Knodel, *Saint-John Perse*, pp. 71–75.

5. M. Parent, *Saint-John Perse et quelques devanciers*, p. 215.

6. For further information on the symbolic value of piercing and cutting weapons, see J.-P. Richard, *Onze études sur la poésie moderne*, pp. 44–46; G. Durand, *Les structures anthropologiques de l'imaginaire*, pp. 166–69.

7. See C. Vigée, *Révolte et Louanges*, p. 19.

8. See G. Durand, *Les structures anthropologiques de l'imaginaire*, pp. 127–86.

9. For the liturgical meaning of the lamp, the bee, and the pheasant, see M. Parent, *Saint-John Perse et quelques devanciers*, pp. 231–33.

Chapter Five

1. The ritual symbolism of the tree is discussed in Sir James Frazer, *The Golden Bough* (Chapters IX, XXV, XXVII, XL) and in Mircéa Eliade, *Traité d'histoire des religions* (Chapters II, VIII). The customs of decking a May tree with various ornaments and replacing it by a fresh tree one year later, or of burning a strawman to restore fertility may have influenced the basic symbolism of *Winds*.

2. A pun may be intended here, since *ruelles* may refer either to the alleys where precious books and documents have been thrown by a revolutionary mob, or to the bedchambers where the literary-minded *Précieuses* entertained their admirers.

3. In *Honneur à Saint-John Perse*, p. 355.

4. G. Bounoure, in *Winds*, pp. 244–45.

Chapter Six

1. In *Honneur à Saint-John Perse*, pp. 665–67. The unidentified quotations given in the following section are taken from this letter.

2. H. Nemerov, *Poetry and Fiction: Essays*, p. 372.

3. See G. Durand, *Les structures anthropologiques de l'imaginaire*, pp. 340–45.

4. In *Honneur à Saint-John Perse*, p. 666.

5. A. Knodel, *Saint-John Perse*, p. 143; A. Henry, *Amers de Saint-John Perse*, p. 16; C. Roy, R. Kemp, Aragon, in *Honneur à Saint-John Perse*, pp. 492, 493, 582–83.

6. The "man in the tale" is Ulysses spurning Calypso's offer of immortality (*Odyssey*, Book V). The phrase "I will exhaust the road of mortal man" is reminiscent of Pindar's *Third Pythian Ode*. Pindar recounts how Asklepios met his death. At the request of Artemis, Asklepios brought Hippolytus back to life. In his anger, Zeus instantly killed both with a thunderbolt. Pindar draws the moral: "Dear soul of mine, seek not after immortality, but exhaust the realm of the possible."

7. Pascal, *Pensées;* Lamartine, "L'Homme," *Méditations*.

8. The expression "the human phrase" recurs in *Winds* (IV, 4), in the letter on the thematic structure of *Seamarks*, and in the acceptance speech upon the award of the Nobel Prize.

9. Rimbaud also defined poetry as the conquest of the unknown (Letter to P. Demeny, May 15, 1871). The "greater Orb" has a poetic equivalent in Rimbaud's *Voyelles* ("O, suprême clairon plein des strideurs étranges . . ."). For Pre-Socratic philosophers, the sphere represented the unity and perfection of Being.

10. See *Two Addresses*, pp. 11, 13.

11. In *Honneur à Saint-John Perse*, p. 666.

12. A. Knodel, *Saint-John Perse*, pp. 130–31.

13. *Exile*, III; *Winds*, IV, 6; *Seamarks*, *Strophe*, IX, 1. The remarks which follow are based on Saint-John Perse's own commentary of *Seamarks* (in *Honneur à Saint-John Perse*, pp. 665–67). Similarities between Saint-John Perse's views and the theories of Bergson or Teilhard de Chardin have already been indicated. It is quite possible, however, that Saint-John Perse's vision of human destiny was influenced by earlier sources (Hegel, for instance).

Chapter Seven

1. *Honneur à Saint-John Perse*, p. 667.

2. C. Hemley, "Onward and Upward," *The Hudson Review*, Summer 1962, p. 314.

3. In this manifesto, André Breton also listed Sainte-John Perse among those poets in whom he recognized affinities with the spirit of surrealism: "*Saint-John Perse est surréaliste à distance.*"

4. See G. Durand, *Les structures anthropologiques de l'imaginaire*, pp. 127–86.

5. This is the essence of Saint-John Perse's citation for the Nobel Prize (*Honneur à Saint-John Perse*, pp. 641–43).

6. See *Honneur à Saint-John Perse*, p. 52; P. Claudel, *Oeuvres en prose*, pp. 1482–83. When asked: "Do you believe in God?," Saint-John Perse gave this answer: "No, if you mean by that belonging to a definite Church; but I am a spiritualist. I do not think that one can negate a first principle, which, if you wish, I call God." (Unpublished interview with Claudine Chonez, July 1971). Since *Chronique*, the main poem published by Saint-John Perse has been a fragment of a much longer poem, *Chanté par Celle qui fut là* (*La Nouvelle Revue Française*, 1er janvier 1969, pp. 1–5). The title is clearly reminiscent of the verse "Favor for Her who was there," in the *Strophe* of *Seamarks* (IX, 4). The poem is sung by the Woman to her Lover. It celebrates the rhythms of nature, the permanence of man through the vicissitudes of history, the integration of death in the ceremony of life.

Chapter Eight

For this chapter, the following indications will be given in the text: *Poetry* and *Dante*, referring to the text of the *Two Addresses* listed in the bibliography; *Honneur à Saint-John Perse* will be referred to as *Honneur*.

1. "Léon-Paul Fargue, poète," *La Nouvelle Revue Française*, 1er septembre 1963, p. 204.

2. *Ibid.*, pp. 208–9.

3. "Sacre d'un deuil," *Vogue*, February 1, 1964, p. 145.

4. *Winds*, IV, 6; *Seamarks*, *Strophe*, IX, 1.

5. A. MacLeish, "A Note on Alexis Saint-Léger Léger," *Poetry,* March 1942, p. 333.

6. "Léon-Paul Fargue, poète," *La Nouvelle Revue Française,* 1er août 1963, pp. 198–99.

7. Unpublished interview with Claudine Chonez (July 1971).

8. C. Gali, "Quatre heures avec Saint-John Perse," *Arts,* 2–8 novembre 1960.

9. S. K. Langer, *Philosophy in a New Key,* p. 100.

10. J.-P. Richard, *Onze études sur la poésie moderne,* pp. 31–66.

11. *Exile,* VI; *Rains,* III; *Winds,* III, 1, 4.

12. *Honneur à Saint-John Perse,* p. 666. Compare the long poems *Winds* and *Seamarks* and the four-line poem on lightning in *Honneur à Saint-John Perse,* p. 888.

13. "Léon-Paul Fargue, poète," *La Nouvelle Revue Française,* 1er septembre 1963, p. 406.

14. *Honneur à Saint-John Perse,* pp. 657–58; "Face aux Lettres françaises. 1909," *La Nouvelle Revue Française,* mai 1951, p. 83; "Leon-Paul Fargue, poète," *La Nouvelle Revue Française,* 1er septembre 1963, pp. 413–14; *Seamarks, Invocation.*

15. R. Caillois, *Poétique de Saint-John Perse,* p. 56.

16. "Léon-Paul Fargue, poète," *La Nouvelle Revue Française,* 1er août 1963, p. 198.

17. C. Gali, "Quatre heures avec Saint-John Perse," *Arts,* 2–8, novembre 1960.

18. "Hommage à la mémoire de Rabindranath Tagore," *La Nouvelle Revue Française,* 1er novembre 1961, p. 868.

19. "Silence pour Claudel," *La Nouvelle Revue Française,* 1er septembre 1955, p. 389.

20. "Face aux Lettres françaises. 1909," *La Nouvelle Revue Française,* mai 1951, pp. 77, 79.

21. C. Gali, "Quatre heures avec Saint-John Perse, *Arts,* 2–8 novembre 1960.

22. "Face aux Lettres françaises. 1909," *La Nouvelle Revue Française,* mai 1951, pp. 77–78.

Selected Bibliography

PRIMARY SOURCES

A. Poetic works (in French)

Oeuvre poétique. 2 vols. Paris: Gallimard, 1960 (I. Eloges. La Gloire des Rois. Anabase. Exil. Index bibliographique. II. Vents. Amers. Chronique. Index bibliographique).

"Des Villes sur trois modes." *Pan.* no. 4, juillet-août 1908. Pp. 189–191 (Rare; copy available at Fonds Doucet, Bibliothèque Sainte-Geneviève, Paris).

Unpublished translation of Pindar's *Pythian Odes* (extracts in E. Noulet, "Le ton dans la poésie de Saint-John Perse," *Synthèses,* septembre-octobre 1968. Pp. 10–20.

"Poème" (Pour Valery Larbaud). *Intentions,* novembre 1922. Pp. 52–53. (Reproduced in *Honneur à Saint-John Perse,* pp. 651–52).

Untitled adaptation of T. S. Eliot's poem "The Hollow Men." *Commerce,* hiver 1924, unpaginated.

Four-line poem inspired by a Zen painting [1961]. Reproduced in *Honneur à Saint-John Perse,* p. 809.

L'Ordre des Oiseaux. Paris: "Au Vent d'Arles," 1962. With twelve color etchings by Georges Braque.

"Chanté par Celle qui fut là." *La Nouvelle Revue Française,* 1er janvier 1969. Pp. 1–5.

"Chant pour un équinoxe." *La Nouvelle Revue Française,* septembre 1971, pp. 1–2.

B. Poetic works in bilingual editions (French and English)

Eloges and Other Poems. New York: Bollingen Series LV, Pantheon Books, 1956. Translation by Louise Varèse. Bibliography.

Anabasis. New York: Harcourt, Brace and Co., 1949. Translation by T. S. Eliot. Prefaces by T. S. Eliot, Valery Larbaud, Hugo von Hofmannsthal, Giuseppe Ungaretti. Bibliography.

Exile and Other Poems. New York: Bollingen Series XV, Pantheon Books, 1949. Translation by Denis Devlin. Notes by Archibald MacLeish, Roger Caillois, Alain Bosquet. Bibliography.

Winds. New York: Bollingen Series XXXIV, Pantheon Books, 1953. Translation by Hugh Chisholm. Notes by Paul Claudel, Gaëtan Picon, Albert Béguin, Gabriel Bounoure. Bibliography.

Seamarks. New York: Bollingen Series LXVII, Pantheon Books, 1958. Translation by Wallace Fowlie. Bibliography.

Chronique. New York: Bollingen Series LXIX, Pantheon Books, 1961. Translation by Robert Fitzgerald. Bibliography.

Birds. New York: Bollingen Series LXXXII, Pantheon Books, 1966. Translation by Wallace Fowlie. Bibliography. Reproduction of four etchings by Georges Braque.

Chanté par Celle qui fut là. Princeton: Princeton University Press, 1970. Translation by Richard Howard.

C. Tributes

"Lettre sur Jacques Rivière." *La Nouvelle Revue Française,* avril 1925. Pp. 455–62.

"Briand." Commemorative speech given at New York University, 1942. In *Honneur à Saint-John Perse,* pp. 716–22.

"Face aux lettres françaises. 1909. *La Nouvelle Revue Française,* mai 1951. Pp. 75–86 [Tribute to André Gide].

"Message pour Valery Larbaud." *Les Cahiers de la Pléiade,* automne 1951-printemps 1952. Pp. 9–14.

"Poète, Schéhadé." *Cahiers de la Compagnie Madeleine Renaud-Jean-Louis Barrault,* 41e cahier (1954). P. 23.

"Silence pour Claudel." *La Nouvelle Revue Française,* septembre 1955. Pp. 387–91.

"Pour Adrienne Monnier." *Le Mercure de France,* janvier 1956. Pp. 11–12.

"Larbaud ou l'honneur littéraire." *La Nouvelle Revue Française,* septembre 1957. Pp. 387–400.

"Message pour Giuseppe Ungaretti." In G. Ungaretti, *Il Taccuino del Vecchio.* Milano: Mondadori, 1960. P. 103.

"Hommage à la mémoire de Rabindranath Tagore." *La Nouvelle Revue Française,* octobre 1961. Pp. 868–71.

"Carta de Saint-John Perse," *Sur,* mayo–junio 1962. P. 72. [Tribute to Borges]

"Léon-Paul Fargue, poète." *La Nouvelle Revue Française,* août 1963. Pp. 197–210; septembre 1963. Pp. 406–22.

"A ceux des Cahiers du Sud." *Cahiers du Sud,* LVI, nos. 373–74, septembre-octobre-novembre 1963. Pp. 3–5.

"Grandeur de Kennedy." In *Le Monde,* 20 novembre 1963.

"Sacre d'un deuil." *Vogue,* February 1964. Pp. 144–45 [Tribute to the widow of President Kennedy].

"Pierre levée." *Derrière le miroir,* nos. 144–45–46, mai 1964. Unpaginated. [Tribute to Braque]

"Dante." Address for the inauguration of the International Congress in Florence on the occasion of the seventh centenary of Dante (1965). French text with English translation by Robert Fitzgerald in *Two Addresses* (New York: Bollingen Series LXXXVI, Pantheon Books, 1966).

"Alain Bosquet en notre temps," *Marginales,* avril 1969. P. 3.

"À René Char." *L'Herne, Cahier no. 15* (1971), p. 17.

D. Acceptance speeches.

Acceptance speech upon receipt of the American Academy of Arts and Letters' Award of Merit Medal (1950). In *Honneur à Saint-John Perse,* p. 635.

Acceptance speech upon the award of the *Grand Prix National des Lettres* (1959). In *Honneur à Saint-John Perse,* p. 640.

"Poésie." Acceptance speech upon the award of the Nobel Prize for Literature (1960). In *Honneur à Saint-John Perse,* pp. 644–46. French text and English translation by W. H. Auden in *Two Addresses.* New York: Bollingen Series LXXXVI, Pantheon Books, 1966.

E. Letters and documents

Only letters and documents which do not appear in *Honneur à Saint-John Perse* have been listed here.

Unpublished letter dated Pau, March 10, 1911. Extracts in E. Noulet, "Le ton dans la poésie de Saint-John Perse," *Synthèses,* septembre-octobre 1968. P. 15.

Unpublished letter to Archibald MacLeish, dated 9 September 1941, accompanying manuscript and typescript of *Exil.* Fragment quoted in A. Knodel, *Saint-John Perse,* p. 97.

Letter to Octavio Barreda [1949]. *Et Caetera,* VII, enero-marzo 1961. Facsimile inserted between pp. 16–17.

Letter to Paul Claudel, dated Jan. 7, 1950, in Paul Claudel, *Oeuvres en Prose.* Paris: Gallimard, 1965. Pp. 1482–83.

Extracts from three letters to the publisher of *L'Ordre des Oiseaux.* Anonymous brochure of the exhibit held at the Bibliothèque Nationale from December 17, 1962, to January 17, 1963.

F. Interviews

"Une journée à la villa 'Les Vigneaux.' " Interview with P. Mazars for *Le Figaro Littéraire,* 5 novembre 1960. In *Honneur à Saint-John Perse,* pp. 618–23.

"Quatre heures avec St.-J. Perse." Interview with C. Gali, *Arts* 2–8 novembre 1960.

Unpublished interview with Claudine Chonez [July 1971]. Courtesy of Claudine Chonez.

G. Other texts and documents

This category includes only the texts and documents pertaining to Alexis Leger's diplomatic career. A detailed listing is provided in the "Annexe" of *Honneur à Saint-John Perse*. The bibliography which Saint-John Perse compiled for the Library of Congress may also be listed here:

A Selection of Works for an Understanding of World Affairs since 1914 (Washington: Library of Congress, 1944).

SECONDARY SOURCES

A. Critical works on Saint-John Perse

Special mention must be made of *Honneur à Saint-John Perse*. Gallimard, 1965. This impressive and indispensable work contains nearly one hundred and fifty articles, essays, notes, and tributes. Important texts, speeches, and letters by Saint-John Perse are also included.

BOSQUET, ALAIN. *Saint-John Perse*. Paris: Seghers, 1953. Revised edition: 1967. Introductory essay, selected texts, bibliography.

CAILLOIS, ROGER. *Poétique de Saint-John Perse*. Paris: Gallimard, 1954. Excellent study of the poet's techniques.

CHARPIER, JACQUES. *Saint-John Perse*. Paris: Gallimard, 1962. Detailed biography, critical essay, selected texts, bibliography.

GUERRE, PIERRE. *Saint-John Perse et l'Homme*. Paris: Gallimard, 1955. General classification of Saint-John Perse's themes.

HENRY, ALBERT. *AMERS de Saint-John Perse. Une poésie du mouvement*. Neuchâtel: Editions de la Baconnière, 1963.

KNODEL, ARTHUR. *Saint-John Perse. A Study of his Poetry*. Edinburgh: Edinburgh University Press, 1966. A full-scale study. Extremely well documented.

LORANQUIN, ALBERT. *Saint-John Perse*. Paris: Gallimard, 1963. Aims at "placing" Saint-John Perse in the evolution of modern French poetry. Not always well informed.

MURCIAUX, CHRISTIAN. *Saint-John Perse*. Paris: Editions universitaires, 1960. General survey of the poet's life and works.

PARENT, MONIQUE. *Saint-John Perse et quelques devanciers*. Paris: Klincksieck, 1960. Stylistic study of Saint-John Perse's poetry.

SAILLET, MAURICE. *Saint-John Perse, Poète de Gloire*. Paris: Mercure de France, 1952. Brief studies of the main poems. Some glaring misinterpretations.

B. Articles and essays on Saint-John Perse

BOUNOURE, GABRIEL. "Saint-John Perse and Poetic Ambiguity," in *Winds*. New York: Bollingen Series XXXIV, Pantheon Books, 1953. Pp. 242–47.

BROMBERT, VICTOR. "Perse's Avian Order," *The Hudson Review*, Autumn 1966. Pp. 494–97. Excellent review of *Birds*.

CARMODY, FRANCIS. "Saint-John Perse, Several Oriental Sources," *Comparative Literature Studies*, vol. II, no. 2, 1965. Pp. 125–51. Lists oriental motifs which Saint-John Perse might have found in Plutarch, Herodotus, Ammianus Marcellinus, Strabo.

CHAPIN, KATHERINE GARRISON. "Saint-John Perse. Notes on Some Poetic Contrasts," *Sewanee Review*, vol. LX, no. 1, 1952. Pp. 65–81. Contrasts the "aristocratic" and the "primitive" personalities of the poet.

————. "Saint-John Perse. Some Notes on a French Poet and an Epic Poem," *Sewanee Review*, vol. LXVI, no. 1, Winter 1958. Pp. 33–43. Sound reading of *Winds*.

CHARPIER, JACQUES. "Saint-John Perse and the Fertile Woman." *Yale French Studies*, no. 11, 1953. Pp. 101–5. Contrasts the image of Woman in the works of Saint-John Perse with other views of Woman in the Western tradition.

COLT, BYRON. "Saint-John Perse," *Accent*, vol. XX, no. 3, Summer 1960. Pp. 158–69. On the motif of primitive magic in Saint-John Perse.

GARAUDY, ROGER. "Saint-John Perse," in *D'un réalisme sans rivages*. Paris: Plon, 1963. Pp. 115–49. Favorable criticism from a well-known Marxist scholar.

GIRARD, RENE. "*Winds* and Poetic Experience," *The Berkeley Review*, vol. I, no. 1, Winter 1956. Pp. 46–52. A brilliant interpretation of *Winds*.

GUICHARNAUD, JACQUES. "Vowels of the Sea: *Amers*, by Saint-John Perse," *Yale French Studies*, no. 21, 1958. Pp. 72–82. Stresses the "secular mysticism" of Saint-John Perse.

HEMLEY, CECIL. "Onward and Upward," *The Hudson Review*, Summer 1962. Pp. 314–17. On the vision of history presented in *Chronique*, which the reviewer finds depressing.

KNODEL, ARTHUR. "On approaching a difficult poet," *The Berkeley Review*, vol. I, no. 1, Winter 1956. Pp. 26–33. On the nature and causes of obscurity in the works of Saint-John Perse.

————. "Towards an Understanding of *Anabase*," *Publications of the*

Modern Language Association, June 1964. Pp. 329–43. Detailed exegesis.

LITTLE, J. ROGER. "Elements of the Jason-Medea myth in *Exil* by Saint-John Perse," *The Modern Language Review*, vol. LXI, 1966. Pp. 422–425. Studies possible allusions to the myth.

————. "The Image of the Threshold in the Poetry of Saint-John Perse," *The Modern Language Review*, vol. 64, no. 4, October 1969. Pp. 777–92. On the ritual and metaphysical significance of the threshold symbol.

————. "Language as Imagery in Saint-John Perse," *Forum for Modern Language Studies*, vol. VI, no. 2, April 1970. Pp. 127–39. On significant motifs (space, the bee, the sea).

————. "Une image de la dialectique mouvement-stasis dans l'*Anabase* de Saint-John Perse," *Revue des Sciences Humaines*, avril-juin 1971. Pp. 229–35. Contrasts the tree and grass motifs.

MACLEISH, ARCHIBALD. "A Note on Alexis Saint-Léger Léger," *Poetry*, vol. LIX, no. 6, March 1942. Pp. 330–37. Contains the English translation of a personal letter to Archibald MacLeish.

MAXENCE, MICHEL. "Saint-John Perse ou la tentation de la démesure," *Tel Quel*, no. 4, Automne 1961. Pp. 57–64. Accuses Saint-John Perse of attempting to replace reality by Platonic archetypes, history by myth, and contemporary decadence by a false archaism.

NEMEROV, HOWARD. "The Golden Compass Needle," in *Poetry and Fiction: Essays*. New Brunswick: Rutgers University Press, 1963. Pp. 366–81. Unfavorable criticism of *Seamarks*, but some perceptive comments on its ritual structure.

NOULET, EMILIE. "Saint-John Perse," in *Alphabet critique*. Bruxelles: Presses Universitaires de Bruxelles, 1966, vol. IV. Pp. 20–71. Reviews and essays.

————. "Le ton dans la poésie de Saint-John Perse," *Synthèses*, septembre-octobre 1968. Pp. 10–20. Compares the tone in *Seamarks* and in Pindar's *Odes*, making use of unpublished documents: a letter and extracts from Saint-John Perse's translation of Pindar, with original notes.

PARENT, MONIQUE. "Le thème de l'orage dans *Exil* de Saint-John Perse," *Boletim de filologia*, vol. XIX, 1960. Pp. 209–16.

PAULHAN, JEAN. "Enigmes de Perse," in *Oeuvres complètes* (Paris: Cercle du Livre Précieux, 1969), vol. IV. Pp. 163–94. The enigmas are three: an epic without a hero, a celebration without assured motivation, a rhetoric without language.

POGGIOLI, RENATO. "The Poetry of Saint-John Perse," in *The Spirit and the Letter*. Cambridge: Harvard University Press, 1965. Pp. 229–53. Penetrating study of the poet's work up to *Winds*.

RAINE, KATHLEEN. "Saint-John Perse, Poet of the Marvellous," *En-*

counter, vol. XXIX, no. 4, October 1967. Pp. 51–61. Contains a vivid evocation of the author's meetings with Saint-John Perse.

RICHARD, JEAN-PIERRE. "Saint-John Perse," in *Onze études sur la poésie moderne.* Paris: Editions du Seuil, 1966. Pp. 31–66. Major study of the poet's dominant motifs. Only a portion of this essay is included in *Honneur à Saint-John Perse.*

ROY, CLAUDE. "Saint-John Perse," in *Descriptions critiques.* Paris: Gallimard, 1949. Pp. 133–45. Favorable criticism from a Marxist viewpoint.

SENGHOR, LEOPOLD SEDAR. "Saint-John Perse, ou poésie du royaume d'enfance," in *Liberté I.* Paris: Editions du Seuil, 1964. Pp. 334–353. Relates the vision of Saint-John Perse to the theories of Teilhard de Chardin. Includes good study of the poet's use of rhythms, sounds, and symbols.

SRINIVASA IYENGAR, K. R. "St.-John Perse's *Anabase:* A Study," *The Aryan Path,* vol. XXXIII, no. 1, January 1962. Pp. 15–18; no. 2, February 1962. Pp. 57–62. A reading of the poem by an oriental scholar.

WEINBERG, BERNARD. "Saint-John Perse. *Anabase,*" in *The Limits of Symbolism.* Chicago & London: The University of Chicago Press, 1966. Pp. 365–419. A detailed exegesis of *Anabasis.*

C. Other works cited.

BONAPARTE, PRINCESSE MARIE. *Psychanalyse et anthropologie.* Paris: Presses Universitaires de France, 1952.

CAMPBELL, JOSEPH. *The Masks of God.* New York: The Viking Press. 3 vols. 1959–1964.

DURAND, GILBERT. *Les structures anthropologiques de l'imaginaire.* Paris: Presses Universitaires de France, 1963.

ELIADE, MIRCEA. *Traité d'histoire des religions.* Paris: Payot, 1964.

FRAZER, SIR JAMES. *The Golden Bough* (abridged edition). New York: The Macmillan Company, 1947.

LANGER, SUSANNE K. *Philosophy in a New Key.* New York: The New American Library of World Literature, 1948.

MALRAUX, ANDRE. *Les Noyers de l'Altenburg.* Paris: Gallimard, 1948.

———. *Les Voix du Silence.* Paris: Gallimard, 1951.

Index